MW00852484

Title Page

The Astrological Foundation Of The Christ Myth, Book Three

By Malik H. Jabbar

Published By

Rare Books Distributor

PO Box 13975

Columbus, Oh 43213

http://www.TheChristMyth.com

A

Copyright

B

Table Of Diagrams

Introduction

A Guide to The Purposes And Focus Of This Book

What is the True Meaning and Purpose of biblical scriptures?

My goal in writing "The Astrological Foundation Of The Christ Myth, Book Three" is to answer and *prove* the answer to the aforementioned question. I have already explained in Books One and Two that Religion is the evolutionary child of Astronomy, Astrology and Myth.

In Book Three, we shall go to great lengths to prove beyond any reasonable doubt that this hypothesis is completely accurate and provable. I have stated that *Religious Scripture is* actually *a Registry* of astronomical phenomena in a mythological format. Astronomy is a science and as such, is subject to scientific means of proof and deduction.

WITNESS MY QUOTE FROM BOOK TWO:

"Ancient Mythology was the rendering of scientific astronomy in a mythological format. Mythology symbolizes the movements of the heavenly bodies within the cosmos. Astronomy deals with charting the cycles of all the entities within the cosmos. The Prophecy that prevails in Mythology and religion is a result of this charting. **Of course a Prophecy**, when delivered in a *personified* religious format, seems to be the miraculous foretelling of human events. But, in it's Original form; the Prophecy did

not pertain to future human activity. *The Prophecy pertained to the future movements of celestial entities.*

I often refer to Astrology/Mythology as Scientific, because it is absolutely that. Astrology/Mythology is based on the Science of Astronomy. **To clarify my point,** *let us now define Science. Science Begins with Observation. The scientists seek to detect patterns , laws, and cycles in that which is being observed. In this case, the Starry Heavens.* **Secondly** *, the Scientists Records the patterns , laws, and cycles that they have successfully detected , from their initial observations.* **Thirdly,** *the scientists renew their observations, and compare the results of their continued studies with the records of their past observations. When the scientists are successful , in their attempts to identify consistently repetitive cycles, they then, on this basis, record their conclusions as to scientific facts.*

This registry of scientific conclusions *then serves as a model by which scientists can accurately predict the recurrence of certain events based on their records of established cycles. The ancient Astronomers consequently wrote predictions as to future motions within the cosmos based on their recorded observations.* **Since the Astronomers/Astrologers used a mythological format** *to record their findings, their predictions of future cycles* **were transformed** *into the Prophecies of the Deities, their future conquests, intrigues, wars, and defeats.*

So when **Religion evolved from mythology,** *the chain continued. The Predictions of the scientific Astronomers (Astrologers/Mathematicians), that became the Oracles of Fabled Deities,* **when recorded under mythological headings,** *continued as the Prophecies of Messengers from God,* **in their Religious Format"**

Astronomy is a science and is subject to mathematical proofs and analysis. Consequently, if my proposition is correct i.e. that the bible is, in fact, Astronomy written in a mythological format – *it must also hold true that the bible[1] (like astronomy) is also subject to scientific and mathematical analysis.*

And furthermore, the method that I shall use to prove this Contention: that the bible is a symbolical rendering of astronomy will be by providing Scientific, Mathematical and Astronomical Interpretations to various portions of the bible. These Interpretations will be reinforced and substantiated with Fact, not unsupported speculation.

These interpretations are *not* speculative or opinionated, but rather are based on methods of scientific deduction (i.e. unbiased, methodological, dispassionate) *and* are therefore mathematically verifiable. **Math is a Universal Truth.** *Of Course, Anyone can offer an interpretation based on conjecture and/or opinion,* but when it comes to defining Universal Truth, opinions and guesses will not suffice. **My interpretations are mathematically verifiable** [2]– this is the proof of their accuracy. The Ancients wrote religious scriptures in a coded form. Our mission within this Book is to transform this code into plain language, and this we shall do, scientifically.

---

[1] This application is not restricted to the Christian bible but applies to the "bibles" of all the major religions, of ancient origin or genesis. They all follow the same general rules of cosmic symbolism.

[2] I will draw parallels between various biblical scriptures and astronomical phenomena; and in course unveil mathematical correspondences between the two (astronomy and scripture).

OUR BIBLE IS NOT AN ORIGINAL DOCUMENT.
All of our modern Religious Text are actually Edited versions of Ancient scriptures; Ancient scriptures that have no traceable origin. Our Bibles, Korans, Vedas and religious scriptures of whatever stripe, were fashioned into Books by the Religious Organizations that claimed these Books as their Inspiration. These Books were, for the major part at least, developed from Ancient Text, Folklore, Oral Myths and Tales that have no traceable origin.
The myths and tales of the bible are as old as recorded time itself. Various cultures have edited the ancient text to Match their geographical locations and timeline, and they have created False (Mythological) histories by inserting themselves (their tribes, nations or races) into their revised versions. Much of what the general public views as history is actually mythology. Our scholars have been telling us for years that the origins of many ancient societies are shrouded in myth and fable. *We have noticed also* that many National myths seem to convey a Common theme, for example the claim to Demigod status for the royal family is very common.
It is extremely important that we understand this one Vital Point; that our modern religious scriptures are, in fact, the Edited Versions of Myths and Fables that originated in (what we consider)Prehistory. One of the major keys to the

correct interpretation of biblical myths is the proper *understanding of the Impetus* that caused its' (myth) creation (both oral and written) in the first place. **Our ability to decode the ancient myths is immeasurably enhanced** when we possess an understanding of the *factors that Motivated the Ancients* to create and record these Tales. That Motivation was the *Need* for **Correct Timekeeping!**

Time! Time! Time! – This term "Time" goes to the Root of the matter. <u>Time is Life and Life is Time</u>. The greatest help (aid to the correct understanding of the Gnosis) that my *Spiritual Father* ever gave to me was his reference to religion as the **Theology Of Time**. Time has no beginning or ending, it is omnipresent – and without Time Nothing that Is would Be. Time is an Expanding Force that *cannot Stop Expanding*. **Time requires** *Motion* and the Measurement of Time requires *Demarcation*. The Creation referred to in the Bible is actually the *creation of methods of Time measurement*. We will cover this subject in the First chapter of this Book.

Time was the most important factor affecting the existence of Early (primitive, *Recovering* civilization) Man. The correct measurement of Time was absolutely vital to the survival of Primitive humankind. Whether they lived or died, starved or froze to death was intricately tied with correct Time measurement. Planting had to be done at the proper Time of the year, likewise the harvesting, also migration and hunting and building. Storage of Food stuffs was determined by correct measurement of the seasonal cycles, also the migratory habits of various animals, that were slaughtered to supply food and clothing and shoes etc, were all connected to cycles of Time.

If we Contemplate the Importance of proper Timekeeping in the struggle of Early Humanity, to **survive** amongst the sometimes hostile forces of nature – *we can easily discern their reasoning* and *see* **that the evolution of a "Religious Culture" that was and is innately connected to Time management was a rational, if not inevitable course**.

I have supplied, in the aforementioned comments, a cursory explanation of Factors that may have motivated early society to formulate their religious traditions so as to reflect intimate connections with Timekeeping. Now as we continue along this line of reasoning, our next Focus should be on the probable methods under which this information (systems of Timekeeping) was preserved and passed on to succeeding generations.

Of course we already know that the chief methods utilized by primitive society to record events and history (accumulated knowledge) was through Pictures, Tales, Festivals and Gestures (coded signs) also symbolic Dancing. **When we consider** the essential and vital importance of correct timekeeping to the daily existence of Ancient Man, *we are able to formulate a rationale* that explains **why** early ***Religious Culture** was intimately connected to **Timekeeping***.

The use of Symbolic rather than literal record keeping is explained by the fact that this **Method of Timekeeping** was maintained and sustained by the *Sacerdotal* and *Ruling* classes of ancient society. **Also** the *need* for record keeping (A Registry of Celestial Cycles) **preceded** *the development of the Science of writing,* hence the *Art of Drawing and Oral Rhythmic Verse (Tales, Myths, Folklore)* was incorporated as methods of recording knowledge in lieu of Written Records. **The myths and fables provided the common people with a spiritual outlet** and guaranteed the preservation of the symbolic knowledge because it was made traditional and celebratory. The various rituals were celebrated with fanatical adherence to Time (seasonal) cycles and precision was guaranteed because failure to be correct might invoke the wrath of the deities. This was the attitude of the common folk, although the ruling classes knew better.

THE BIBLE IS ONLY A PART OF A MUCH LARGER BOOK

The Bible is a Book of books. It consist of several separate compositions that were written (edited) by various authors of diverse demographics. Those who compiled the bible, made their selections of scriptures that were included in the Book, based on the Canons of their church. Several compositions were excluded from the bible for various reasons, but mainly because *those excluded Selections* did not conform or support the Focus, Belief or Purposes of the Editors.

Many, many versions of the bible have been compiled in the last 1800 years or so, and all are *not* identical. The various Editors have Included or Excluded information as they saw fit to do. The most popular English translation of the bible is *The Authorized King James Version,* which is the one that I shall use as a reference for my deciphering of the Gnostic Symbolism. At times, I may refer to other English translations in order to clarify or reinforce a point of scripture.

My interpretations shall be to the point, and concise. Some readers may therefore be inspired to seek more detailed information (verification) from other sources. My desire is to avoid shackling the book with copious footnotes and meticulous details that may be unnecessarily pedantic to the average Truth Seeker. **In my opinion**, excessive details tend to obscure the true focus of a book rather than aid it. Nevertheless, some Interpretations are Intricate, and may require Rereading, but most are very vivid. A Bibliography is provided for aid in further research. I strongly suggest use of the Appendix. Also the Appendix of *"The Astrological Foundation Of The Christ Myth, Book One"* has some very useful information. A good Handbook on astronomy is strongly recommended.

The fact that *All* of the Ancient Scriptures are not contained in the *King James Version* of the bible or in any *One* bible is not important. The KJV contains more Information than anyone could properly decipher in a lifetime. I am very Impressed that the Symbolism has been maintained so well, through it's many translations; from the Hebrew to the Greek to the Latin and into English. The fact that the Gnosis is pretty well intact after 2000 years of multiple Translations and Literary Hanky Panky is remarkable.

I am sometimes bewildered that some reasonably intelligent people have difficulty understanding (accepting) biblical symbolism, even after it is clearly explained and *Proven* to them. I am convinced that this stubbornness is due largely to our *Cultural Programming*. We have been culturally programmed (educated) to recognize or discern Truth. **The accepted method** of analyzing the Validity of a supposition **is by Comparison**; that is we tend to compare the *Unknown quality* (supposition) with the *Known quality* (accepted cultural opinions). If the *Unknown Quality* **Conforms** to the *Known Quality*, then this supposedly indicates a validation of the previously Unknown Quality; but if it (the supposition) does not Conform, we tend to reject it. This method of Comparison works fine, **if our Criterion** (accepted cultural opinions) **are Valid** and Accurate. **However,** if *our Basic Assumptions are Flawed*, it follows that any and all

determinations that are **derived**, based on *invalid premises (that we have traditionally accepted, without critical investigation)* will probably be the **wrong conclusions**.
The best Analysis is an Independent analysis, without Preconceived notions. The Best (evaluating) tool at our disposal is our *Ability to Reason*. Rational thinking will work wonders if we allow it free reign, but that's easier said than done. **Check out the Root Definition of the word "Religion", from the Latin** – it is defined: to tie down, to bind.
The fables of the bible fit into the same category as the ancient Greek Myths, the Roman Myths, the Hindu Myths etc. **The bible is composed of Hebrew Myths and Christian Myths** – that is the way you Must view this issue, if you are sincerely seeking clarity. The bible is Not Sacred; it was **not** written by god and it is not a *divinely* inspired revelation. **The bible is a Book of Science** (a Registry of Astronomical Phenomena) written in a Mythological Format. A Critical analysis of biblical scripture will not Ring with success unless it is done Dispassionately. **If your critique** is geared at proving some Preconceived Notion, that you intend to hold on to **Regardless** of your findings (even though the resulting information may contradict your established assumptions) – then you *may* be unreasonably Biased and your results will be *skewed*, in my opinion. **Fear of the Truth will**

keep you from recognizing or accepting the Truth. *I define Truth* as that which is naturally and mathematically verifiable. If we don't possess the skills to pin the Truth down mathematically, then our most positive recourse is to resort to Reason. The Truth tends to be Reasonable in most cases.

BIBLICAL (ASTRONOMICAL) SYMBOLISM IS APPROXIMATE AND THEREFORE MUST BE ADJUSTED FROM TIME TO TIME

I must once again call your attention to an issue that I raised in Book Two concerning prophecy.

Witness my quote from Book Two:

"Ancient Mythology was the rendering of scientific astronomy in a mythological format. Mythology symbolizes the movements of the heavenly bodies within the cosmos. Astronomy deals with charting the cycles of all the entities within the cosmos. The Prophecy that prevails in Mythology and religion is a result of this charting. Of course a Prophecy, when delivered in a personified religious format, seems to be the miraculous foretelling of human events. But, in it's Original form; the Prophecy did not pertain to future human activity. The Prophecy pertained to the future movements of celestial entities."

I must also reiterate – The bible is a *Registry* of recorded astronomical phenomena written in a mythological format. **The understanding of this One Vital Point is the Key** to the proper deciphering of biblical symbolism. The bible (a book of astronomical symbolism) deals with the recording of astronomical cycles and the Predictions of the reoccurrence of these cycles, also the evolution of major cycles generated by minor cycles. The consequences or purpose of all this is to *operate* and *preserve* a System of progressive Calendrical adjustments throughout time.

The activity of correlating *Time Cycles* **always** produces fractions. The natural cycles of the elements within the cosmos such as the moon, sun, the equinoxes and solstices, sequences of eclipses, revolutions of the planets, comets and all such astronomical activity occur at intervals that cannot be reduced to whole numbers; hence, there is always the need for the *Astronomers* (Priesthood, Biblical Editors) to continually *update and adjust* their calculations, as Time marches on.

The Ancients developed a system that recorded *some* cycles as whole numbers, without regard to the *fractions*, and then at predictable intervals they would adjust their calculations to another whole number of a *greater cycle* that was closer to accuracy. **For example**, although our year is 365 ¼ days long – we disregard the fraction, but at intervals of 4 years we add a whole number (day) and this brings us closer to accuracy in our time keeping.

But actually this adjustment is not accurate; it is simply *closer* to accuracy. The actual year is 365.242199 days long, so 4 times this number produces 1460.968796. So by adding a whole number to our calendar we merely reduce the error to a smaller fraction i.e. .031204 days instead of .242199 days.

However, with every 4 years passing (when we make this adjustment), we are adding incrementally to our error so that eventually the smaller error will exceed the larger error – **And it is this Type of problem that influenced the Priesthood (biblical Editors) to invent a System of Prophecy** that would enable them to convey instructions (for Calendrical adjustments) to succeeding Generations (of the Initiated).

But before I connect this to biblical prophecy, I would like to interject this point about **Festivals.** One of the ways that the Sacerdotal class would handle the problem of calibrating the calendar to a larger cycle, in order to reduce the incremental discrepancies caused by the periodic adjustments of minor cycles, **was this:** They would *calculate the date when* these smaller fractions would accumulate to a whole number (day) which might be 72 years, 360 years, 1440 years, 2160 years or whatever – and they would designate that time (end of the cycle) as a day of celebration, commemorating some Deity or Event, and include this pronouncement in their writings (scriptures) and/or folklore. **So when that day arrived** the Common people would take to the streets in gaiety and celebration of some mythological fancy, while the Priesthood would slink into their Chambers and Observatories – getting on with their work of proper Timekeeping.

The predictions and prophecies about an expected Savior, Avenger, Avatar or divine Messenger and the like were all coded messages sent out, by the Priesthood, to the Initiated and their descendants. This mythology was taken literally by the Common people but the Initiated knew better. Throughout the bible we are warned about a Coming Savior and a dreaded Day of Judgment or a Glorious Day of Deliverance. **All of these -** the expected Savior, Judgment Day and/or Deliverance and the like **are esoteric symbolisms related to adjustments in Timekeeping.**

As I explained above, All adjustments to the calendar (Time Keeping) are temporary and *inexact*, and generate the need for further adjustments – at times, far into the distant future. Some cycles run into thousands of years. So the Priesthood had to develop a method of passing the Word (instructions for future Calendrical adjustments) to succeeding Generations; Generations that would come to life hundreds or thousands of years into the future.

The Method that the Ancients used was to *predict* the *Coming* of a Savior at some distant point in time. **The Mission of the Savior** would be to bring Justice to the World, To Deliver humanity from Bondage, To Chastise people for their Sins, To Destroy the Transgressors, To Mediate and Reconcile the Enmity and Hatred among peoples. **This is Coded Language** used to instruct succeeding Generations (within the circle of the Initiated) as to *When* they must make adjustments to the Calendar. **The Mission of the Savior**

concerns Justice, Deliverance, Transgression, Mediation, Chastisement. All of these Terms relate to the **Correction of Errors**, but not errors in ones social habits as the uninitiated think – but rather Errors in **mathematical computations** that govern proper Time Keeping.

We have already learned, from what I wrote above, that our method of timekeeping (calendar) requires periodic adjustments. The Transgressions that the Savior will come to remedy are not social transgressions but rather mathematical transgressions. The Savior shall Mediate (reconcile) the Errors of computation, He shall make Judgment on the Errors in Time keeping, He shall Destroy the Wrong Doers (Numbers) and replace them with correct Numbers. I could go on and on. **The Savior actually refers to the Priesthood** of the Generation to which the prophecy is directed. The Priesthood[3] (biblical Editors) is the actual Savior that continually Edits and Re-Edits the Scriptures from Generation to Generation throughout history.

The *Coming Savior* is often referred to as a Mediator, Judge, Avenger, Destroyer, Chastiser, Emancipator. All of these words have obvious social implications, but in fact **the words**

---

[3] I use the terms Priesthood and Biblical Editors as a sort of shorthand that actually refers to the Initiated Hierarchy of All religions.

are codes that indicate corrections and adjustments to the mathematical computations that govern correct timekeeping. The year and date that the Savior is destined to arrive is *Always* pegged to the year and date when the calendar must be Updated (Judged, Corrected, Mediated, etc).
Witness this Definition from the Dictionary.com:

mediator one who intervenes between two persons who are at variance, with a view to reconcile them. This word is not found in the Old Testament; but the idea it expresses is found in Job 9:33, in the word "daysman" (q.v.), marg., "umpire." This word is used in the New Testament to denote simply an internuncius, an ambassador, one who acts as a medium of communication between two contracting parties. In this sense Moses is called a mediator in Gal. 3:19. Christ is the one and only mediator between God and man (1 Tim. 2:5; Heb. 8:6; 9:15; 12:24). He makes reconciliation between God and man by his all-perfect atoning sacrifice. Such a mediator must be at once divine and human, divine, that his obedience and his sufferings might possess infinite worth, and that he might possess infinite wisdom and knowlege and power to direct all things in the kingdoms of providence and grace which are committed to his hands (Matt. 28:18; John 5:22, 25, 26, 27); and human, that in his work he might represent man, and be capable of rendering obedience to the law and satisfying the claims of justice (Heb. 2:17, 18; 4:15, 16), and that in his glorified humanity he might be the head of a glorified Church (Rom. 8:29). This office involves the three functions of prophet, priest, and king, all of which are discharged by Christ both in his estate of humiliation and exaltation. These functions are so inherent in the one office that the quality appertaining to each gives character to every mediatorial act. They are never separated in the exercise of the office of mediator.

Source: *Easton's 1897 Bible Dictionary*

Research the definitions of these words; *Mediator, Deliverance, Judgment* and other words that commonly refer to a Savior or his actions and I am sure you will agree that the terms are applicable to the correction of mathematical Errors. *The biblical Editors have used these Terms metaphorically to pass coded messages between each other throughout thousands of years.* This is my Contention, and I think that the facts and Reason support this conclusion better than the alternatives.

Much of this book deals with the deciphering of Calendrical astronomical symbolism that reaffirms this premise.

Malik H. Jabbar

Chapter One - The Astrological Origin Of The Sabbath

Symbolism Of the Six Days Creation, And Seventh Day Of Rest

In The Beginning God Created The Heaven And The Earth

We have been taught, by way of the bible, that God created the Universe in six days and on the seventh day *He Rested.* Furthermore, that this **seventh day (Sabbath) is Holy** and should be set aside for all eternity as a day dedicated to the Creator in Commemoration of his beneficence to us.
See Exodus 20:

8Remember the sabbath day, to keep it holy. 9Six days shalt thou labour, and do all thy work: 10But the seventh day *is* the sabbath of the LORD thy God: *in it* thou shalt not do any work, thou, nor thy son, nor thy daughter, thy manservant, nor thy maidservant, nor thy cattle, nor thy stranger that *is* within thy gates: 11For *in* six days the LORD made heaven and earth, the sea, and all that in them *is*, and rested the seventh day: wherefore the LORD blessed the sabbath day, and hallowed it.

Exodus 31:

12And the LORD spake unto Moses, saying, 13Speak thou also unto the children of Israel, saying, Verily my sabbaths ye shall keep: for it *is* a sign between me and you throughout your generations; that *ye* may know that I *am* the LORD that doth sanctify you. 14Ye shall keep the sabbath therefore; for it *is* holy unto you: **every one that defileth it shall surely be put to death:** for whosoever doeth *any* work therein, that soul shall be cut off from among his people. [15]Six days may work be done; but in the seventh *is* the sabbath of rest, holy to the LORD: whosoever doeth *any* work in the sabbath day, he shall surely be put to death. [16]Wherefore the children of Israel shall keep the sabbath, to observe the sabbath throughout their generations, *for* a perpetual covenant. [17]It *is* a sign between me and the children of Israel for ever: for *in* six days the LORD made heaven and earth, and on the seventh day he rested, and was refreshed. [18]And he gave unto Moses, when he had made an end of communing with him upon mount Sinai, two tables of testimony, tables of stone, written with the finger of God.

Now, we can see from the reading of the biblical verses that I have inserted above, that the Reverence of the Sabbath is a Very Serious matter, according to the scriptures. I'm sure that many of us did not realize that the Punishment for violating the Sabbath is Death!

Actually, All Religious Holidays, including the Sabbath are symbolical representations of Astronomical phenomena. Whenever we observe (celebrate) any religious Holiday or Tradition, whether it be the Sabbath, Christmas, Easter, Baptism or whatever, we are in fact mimicking or acknowledging some astronomical event or interval.

Of course, we have traditionally accepted that the Sabbath and other holidays were observed in commemoration of Godly Interventions into human life, either directly or through his prophets. But since the Bible is Myth and should not be taken Literally, we need to recognize that all of these

19

various Religious ceremonies would be more correctly described as *Astronomical ceremonies*.

Before we can accurately interpret the Astrological Meaning and Origin of the Sabbath, we must first acknowledge that our old traditional Concept is fatally flawed. The Creation story described in the bible is utter nonsense, when taken Literally. The Best way for me to prove this point is to allow you to *Read* this famous Fable (of the worlds creation). But before you Read this biblical passage, Put your Thinking Cap On! Let's be Rational about this, and try our best to study this verse in the same way we might *examine* an Insurance Document or some other type of Contract. If we can get beyond the Fable, Reality (Truth) Awaits Us!

See Genesis 1:

¹In the beginning God created the heaven and the earth. ²And the earth was without form, and void; and darkness was upon the face of the deep. And the Spirit of God moved upon the face of the waters.

³And God said, Let there be light: and there was light. ⁴And God saw the light, that it was good: and God divided the light from the darkness. ⁵And God called the light Day, and the darkness he called Night. And the evening and the morning were the first day.

⁶And God said, Let there be a firmament in the midst of the waters, and let it divide the waters from the waters. ⁷And God made the firmament, and divided the waters which were under the firmament from the waters which were above the firmament: and it was so. ⁸And God called the firmament Heaven. And the evening and the morning were the second day.

⁹And God said, Let the waters under the heaven be gathered together unto one place, and let the dry land appear: and it was so. ¹⁰And God called the dry land Earth; and the gathering together of the waters called he Seas: and God saw that it was good. ¹¹And God said, Let the earth bring forth grass, the herb yielding seed, and the fruit tree yielding fruit after his kind, whose seed is in itself, upon the earth: and it was so. ¹²And the earth brought forth grass, and herb yielding seed after his kind, and the tree yielding fruit, whose seed was in itself, after his kind: and God saw that it was good. ¹³And the evening and the morning were the third day.

¹⁴And God said, Let there be lights in the firmament of the heaven to divide the day from the night; and let them be for signs, and for seasons, and for days, and years: ¹⁵And let them be for lights in the firmament of the heaven to give light upon the earth: and it was so. ¹⁶And God made two great lights; the greater light to rule the day, and the lesser light to rule the night: he made the stars also. ¹⁷And God set them in the firmament of the heaven to give light upon the earth, ¹⁸And to rule over the day and over the night, and to divide the light from the darkness: and God saw that it was good. ¹⁹And the evening and the morning were the fourth day.

²⁰And God said, Let the waters bring forth abundantly the moving creature that hath life, and fowl that may fly above the earth in the open firmament of heaven. ²¹And God created great whales, and every living creature that moveth, which the waters brought forth abundantly, after their kind, and every winged fowl after his kind: and God saw that it was good. ²²And God blessed them, saying, Be fruitful, and multiply, and fill the waters in the seas, and let fowl multiply in the earth. ²³And the evening and the morning were the fifth day.

²⁴And God said, Let the earth bring forth the living creature after his kind, cattle, and creeping thing, and beast of the earth after his kind: and it was so. ²⁵And God made the beast of the earth after his kind, and cattle after their kind, and every thing that creepeth upon the earth after his kind: and God saw that it was good.

²⁶And God said, Let us make man in our image, after our likeness: and let them have dominion over the fish of the sea, and over the fowl of the air, and over the cattle, and over all the earth, and over every creeping thing that creepeth upon the earth. ²⁷So God created man in his own image, in the image of God created he him; male and female created he them. ²⁸And God blessed them, and God said unto them, Be fruitful, and multiply, and replenish the earth, and subdue it: and have dominion over the fish of the sea, and over the fowl of the air, and over every living thing that moveth upon the earth.

²⁹And God said, Behold, I have given you every herb bearing seed, which is upon the face of all the earth, and every tree, in the which is the fruit of a tree yielding seed; to you it shall be for meat. ³⁰And to every beast of the earth, and to every fowl of the air, and to every thing that creepeth upon the earth, wherein there is life, I have given every green herb for meat: and it was so.

³¹And God saw every thing that he had made, and, behold, it was very good. And the evening and the morning were the sixth day. Genesis 2

¹Thus the heavens and the earth were finished, and all the host of them. ²And on the seventh day God ended his work which he had made; and he rested on the seventh day from all his work which he had made. ³And God blessed the seventh day, and sanctified it: because that in it he had rested from all his work which God created and made.

Now that you have *Reread* (with a critical eye) this Tale of the world's Creation, I'm sure that you are bewildered as to how you could have ever accepted this Fable as the Literal Truth.

The Only Truth contained within this Fable is Symbolic Truth.
The Interpretation that Reveals the True origin of the *Sabbath Day* is *very mathematical.* **Therefore**, before I go into a detailed explanation of my premise, **I must first lay a Foundation** by making a general statement that will serve as an overview; and also I must supply additional historical and mathematical information that is not presented in these verses.
The Beginning that is referred to in *Genesis One* **is the Beginning of the Hebrew Cycles of Time Keeping** and the *Methods and Measurements* of that **Lunar System of Time Keeping.** The Seven **Days** (Divisions of Time) are Best[4] understood as *Seven Divisions of the Lunar Month.* **According** to *Genesis One*, on the **First Day of Creation** – God created Light. **Likewise, on the Fourth Day of Creation** – God Again created Light. This *Creation of Light Twice Over* can be viewed as an Indicator of the **Lunar Symbolism.**
Time is measured by Light, and that is why the Editors inserted Two Creations of Light in their prose. It was not a mistake. The *basic system of Time measurement* used by the Ancients (Hebrews and Others) was the *Incremental Light Phases*

---

[4] Actually the Literal Seven Day interpretation applies also, at a certain level of symbolism. But the Seven divisions of the Lunar month leads to a much Greater Unveiling of the Gnosis as it relates to the Twice Over creation of Light.

of the Moon. Hence in *Genesis One* of the bible, **Two Phases of the *Moon Light Cycle* are being described**, and that is why the Editors depicted Two separate Creations of Light.

The First Phase of the **Moon Light Cycle** begins with Impregnation. I have already explained in **Book Two** that Allegorically speaking, the *Conjunctions* (Conjugal symbolism) *of two heavenly bodies* indicates New Birth or Impregnation, the commencement of a Cycle. **The Lunar month commences** with the first sliver (Crescent) of *Moon Light* detectable, after it's Astronomical Impregnation (i.e. when the Sun and Moon are Conjoined). **This** (the visible Crescent) **is the First Creation** of Light that *Genesis One* is referring to. It indicates the Beginning of the *Hebrew Year One* in the Month known as *Tishri*. This took place in the Fall of 3761 BC[5], on Monday (Hebrew calendar reckoning) October 7, 3761 BC at 5 hours 11 minutes and 20 seconds.

The Second Creation Of Light is the Full Moon, which is the Alignment of the Sun, Earth and Moon. **These Two phases of Light** i.e. the *New Moon* and the *Full Moon* are the **Cardinal Points** of Demarcation by which Lunar Time is measured. The First Day (of creation) and the Fourth day (of

---

[5] Get further information on the beginning of the Hebrew Era in your Encyclopedia – look up the Jewish Calendar and Jewish Chronology

creation) are very significant, as can be seen by drawing a straight line[6] between points one and four on a circle (cycle i.e. the moons orbit around the earth). It can be plainly seen in the following Exhibit that *Points* **One** and **Four** are the Positions of Alignment between the Earth, Moon and the Sun. So, when we section the Moon's orbit into six equal parts ("Creation" days) - the first Creation of Light (at the New Moon) and the second Creation of Light (at the Full Moon) are clearly exemplified as the *Demarcation Points* of Light by which Lunar time is reckoned.

---

[6] This imaginary Line represents the Line of alignment for the Sun Moon and Earth, at New Moon or Full Moon

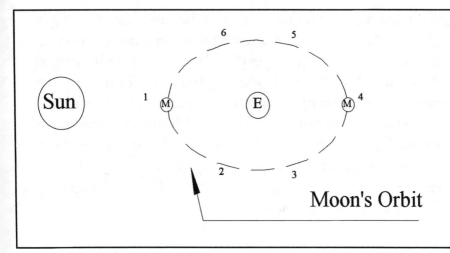

Figure 1: New Moon and Full Moon are the Cardinal Points by which Lunar Timekeeping is governed. Point 1 is the First Creation Of Light and Point 4 is the Second Creation of Light.

Review Of The Hebrew Lunar Calendar

The *Jewish calendar* is the tool by which we may decipher the *Astrological Origin of the Sabbath*. The Creation of the world described in Genesis One is Actually The <u>Year One</u> of the *Jewish Calendar System*.

The starting point of the *Hebrew calendar* is the year 3761 BC. This can be easily verified by research with any good encyclopedia – just look for information on the Jewish calendar, chronology and Jewish festivals.

The *Creation* of the world described in Genesis of the bible is actually the Creation of the *Jewish calendar*, the origin of the Jewish system of Time keeping – the commencement of the Jewish or Hebrew Era. The first day of the world's creation or completion as described in the bible is actually the first Rosh Hashanah of the Hebrew people, their first New Year – Tishri 1 or it's equivalent of 3761 BC. This is historical fact which can be easily verified by research, as I have indicated above.

Not only have the Hebrews supplied us with the year in which their Cycle (creation story of Genesis One) began, but also the Date, The Day, And the Time. This is Marvelous!

The Hebrew Calendar is Lunar solar; this means that the months of the year are *measured* in accordance with the *revolutions of the moon around the earth*. The *years*, in turn, are measured *by mathematical formulas* that are geared to *reconcile* the Lunar cycles with the Solar cycles.
The Solar and Lunar cycles are not naturally in sync. In other words, 12 or 13 Lunar months will not divide evenly into a Tropical year of 365 days. Hence, there the need to periodically reconcile the discrepancy between the two cycles (Lunar and Solar). Failure to Reconcile the lunar year of 353-355 days (Lunar Leap years are 383-385 days) with the

Tropical year of 365-366 days would cause us to loose track of the annual and other cycles; i.e. we would loose track of our place in time. This reconciliation is usually done at intervals of three years or so, *within* a Larger cycle of nineteen years (Metonic Cycle)[7].

The Lunar month alternates between 29 and 30 days to the month. This causes the length of a Regular Lunar year to be 354 days, however, because of mathematical adjustments that are made periodically, the month varies from 353-355 days (383-385 in Lunar leap years). Lunar months and/or years are sometimes referred to as Deficient (353 or 383 days) Regular (354 or 384 days) or Abundant (355 or 385 days).

The Hebrew Day and Date start at 6 PM in the evening. This is an important point to remember. The Hebrew week consist of seven days, beginning with Sunday (starts a 6 PM Saturday evening) as Day one *and* ending with Saturday (starts at 6 PM Friday evening) as Day seven.

The Hebrew New Year starts on Tishri one of the Jewish calendar. This date occurs in the Fall of the year, near the Sun's crossing of the Autumnal Equinox.

---

[7] Search the Appendix for a detailed explanation of cycles.

The Beginning of the Hebrew Lunar month is determined by the appearance of the *First Light* (Crescent) of the New Moon[8] (Birth of the Moon). The Astronomical Phase *of the New Moon* commences when the Moon enters into Conjunction (hence becoming invisible) with the Sun. **The Interval of Time** between the Conjunction (start of invisibility, dark phase) and *the visual* New Moon (i.e. sighting of the Crescent and start of a new month) is *two days five hours eleven minutes and twenty seconds* (in Hebrew terms, 2 days 5 hours 204 Parts[9]). The Ancients calculated the *Mean* length of a Synodic month at *twenty-nine days twelve hours forty-four minutes three and one third seconds* (in Hebrew terms 29 days 12 hours 793 Parts). The Ancients calculated the moon as visible for *twenty-seven days seven hours thirty-two minutes forty-three and one third seconds* (in Hebrew terms 27 days 7 hours 589 Parts) during a month.

---

[8] The first light (crescent moon) is commonly referred to as the New moon, and this is acceptable. Astronomically speaking, the New moon occurs when the Angle between the sun and moon is reduced to "0" degrees. The conjunction of the moon and sun occurs 2 days 5 hours 204 Halakim (2 days 5 hours 11 minutes and 20 seconds) earlier than the birth of the crescent moon, according to the ancient calculations. See Appendix for more information.

[9] Parts are synonymous with Halakim, See appendix for information

The Sabbath Is actually Dedicated to the Moon God[10]

Our purpose, and focus in this chapter of the book, is to show and prove *mathematically* that the **God of Creation** in *Genesis One* is, in fact, an allegorical representation of the **Moon**. Also, that the **Sabbath is actually dedicated to an ancient Moon Deity**. I have already shown, in an earlier paragraph, that *the two creations of Light*, referred to in Genesis One, *represent the two cardinal Light phases of the Moon*, namely the New (Crescent) Moon and the Full Moon. The Calendrical information that I have supplied in the preceding paragraphs is all we need to prove the other points (i.e. the God of Genesis One is a Moon Deity, and that the Sabbath is a Moon Festival, so to speak).

Lets review a portion of the biblical excerpt that I inserted near the beginning of this chapter, from Exodus 31 –" [17]It *is* **a sign between me and the children of Israel for ever: for** *in* **six** *days the* LORD *made heaven and earth*, **and on the** *seventh day he rested*, **and was** *refreshed"*. Now, according to this verse, the Activity ascribed to the Creator God of Genesis is that he #1 Worked on the Creation of the universe for Six Days

---

[10] The Moon Deity is usually feminine, but in some phases of the mythology it is male as in this case.

(Periods of Time) #2 that he Rested in the Seventh Day (Period of Time) #3 that he was Refreshed.

So our Task is to prove a mathematical correlation of these Three activities to the celestial Moon. **Point One:** According to Hebrew religious doctrine – the world was created in 3761 BC on a Monday *(Jewish calendar reckoning)* at 5 hours 204 Halakim[11] *(a Halakim is 3 1/3 seconds)* - which is the second day *(Jewish days start at 6 PM)* of the week at 5 hours and 11 minutes and 20 seconds.

Point Two: We know from the Hebrew astronomical calculations *(and modern calculations too)* that the **Interval of Time** between the Old Moon *(going into darkness)* and the Reemergence of the New Moon *(as a crescent of Light)* **is 2 days 5 hours 204 Halakim**. This equates to 2 days 5 hours 11 minutes and 20 seconds.

Point Three: By subtracting the <u>Interval</u> of the Moon's Darkness (i.e. 2 days 5 hours 204 Halakim) **From the day/date** (Monday[12] at 5 hours 204 Halakim) **of the worlds creation** (which is actually the first year and day of the Jewish calendar cycle) – **the result is 6 PM Friday** (the start of the

---

[11] Our Western Calendar would read Sunday 11 hours 11 minutes 20 seconds PM

[12] Remember that their Monday starts at 6 PM Sunday!

Jewish Sabbath!). **This Means that this date** (Rosh Hoshanah/Creation Day) **in 3761 BC,** *commenced with the New Moon,* and that the *Old Moon was extinguished* at the start of the Jewish Sabbath *(Friday 6PM)* – a time appointed for Rest. The first day of Creation was actually the first New Moon of the Jewish New Year in 3761 BC – and the old moon went to Rest (Darkness) *Exactly* at the start of the Jewish Sabbath (6 PM Friday). **Could this be coincidence?** The Link is undeniable – The first Sabbath[13] was pegged to the Conjunction of the Moon with the Sun, as a result of the Conjunction causing a period of Darkness (REST) to fall over the Moon and consequently the Moon's Work (Light phase) was thereby Terminated by the Greater Light of the Sun i.e. The Moon god's <u>Work of Creation</u> (Light Phase) was Finished. **The *Universe Creation story* of Genesis is a clear description of a Synodic moon cycle**. The Moon cycle starts with the creation of light (New Moon) – **at the midpoint** there is a second creation of light (Full Moon) – **at the final phase** the moon re-enters into darkness (Rest) – and the process completes when the moon light is renewed (Refreshed). This is Vivid!

---

[13] This is the Sabbath (Saturday) that preceded the Hebrew New Year of 3761 BC. That Sabbath commenced simultaneously with the Dark phase of the previous moon cycle

Point Four: God (*actually the Moon Deity*) finishing his creation is synonymous with the Moon Finishing it's last <u>phase of Light</u>. God (Moon Deity) taking a REST was actually the Moon going into a waiting period caused by it's Light being Killed[14] by the Light of the Sun. The Moon was Resting In Darkness, awaiting it's next opportunity to *refresh* it's Light as the New Moon. So the God (*Moon Deity*) being *refreshed* undoubtedly refers to the <u>Refreshing of Light</u> at the beginning of the Next Moon Cycle, which starts (*renews itself*) with the emerging (*refreshed*) crescent of Light (*i.e. New Moon*).

All the parts of this former puzzle fit perfectly. It is Clear that the Hebrews selected Saturday as their Sabbath in commemoration of the Conjunction (conjoining) of the Moon with the Sun. This Conjunction brought Death to their Deity (Moon Light) but it also brought the promise of New Life and Resurrection (of the Moon's Light). The Hebrew injunction that stipulates death as the penalty for violating the Sabbath is simply an allegorical reflection of the Sun Killing the Light of the Moon at the time of the original Jewish Sabbath. **The Foundation of Christian theology** is found right here in this Jewish Symbolism. Jesus Christ is,

---

[14] You may recall the biblical injunction that demanded Death for violating the Sabbath. I think my Interpretation of Killing the Light of the Moon at Conjunction is more sensible than murdering people because they work on a Saturday (Sabbath)

without doubt, a mythological Sun God, but the Origin of the Resurrection myth was actually in Lunar mythology. I think that the Astrological Foundation of the Jewish Sabbath is mathematically clear and indisputable. Genesis One contains a Lot more Symbolism. The First chapter and more of Genesis is actually Bursting At The Seams with Stellar Symbolism, but that is not our Focus, at this Time. Furthermore the Interpretations are much more involved and tedious, so we will move on. However I would like to reinforce my contentions concerning the Resurrection myth a little more. I referred to it in Book Two.

WITNESS QUOTE FROM BOOK TWO:

"The Resurrection of Christ at Easter (the vernal equinox) does not accurately reflect the Solar Mythology. The actual solar death and resurrection takes place at the Winter Solstice.

The Crucifixion of Christ on a Friday and his resurrection on a Sunday (Easter) morning cannot be equated to three days in the grave. This reflects Lunar mythology rather than Solar mythology.

The Lunar mythological cycles vary from the Solar cycles. The Death and Resurrection of the Moon does take place in two days. The cycle of the moon around the earth is measured as a sidereal month (about 28 days) and as a Synodic month (about 30 days). The sidereal month is the shorter of the cycles at less than 28 days. The sidereal month represents the time it takes the moon to revolve around the earth, relative to a distant star as the marker.

The Synodic month measures the revolution relative to the repeated alignment of the moon, earth, and sun, either at the Full moon or the new moon.

The Moon becomes invisible (dies, is buried, or killed, or sheds it's blood) after 28 days into its revolution. When it passes between the earth and the sun, it cannot be seen because of the intense light of the sun. The moon travels about thirteen degrees a day, so there is a span (the moon's path between the earth and sun) of about 27 degrees (2 days), whereas it's light is indistinguishable. When the moon reemerges as a sliver of light known as the New Moon, it has been Mythologically Resurrected; hence this Resurrection of Christ described by the Easter ceremony is clearly Lunar mythology. The Death of Jesus on a Good Friday to a Resurrection on a Sunday Morning is one and a half or two days. This corresponds exactly to the death of the old moon and the birth of the new moon."

Jesus Christ is a Mythological Sun God, but it is clear from the information that I shared from Book Two, that he was also symbolized as a Moon God.
The Death and Resurrection of Jesus (as a Moon God) is symbolized in the Allegory of *Genesis One* also; and with great accuracy when understood.
Jesus being crucified on a Friday and being resurrected on a *Sunday* correlates to the Death (Darkness) of the Moon and it's Resurrection (Rebirth) at the **Molad** of the Jewish calendar cycle. **Molad** is a Jewish term that means Rebirth. It refers to the position of the Moon when it's angle to the Sun has been reduced to "0" degrees. Jewish Doctrine (Calendrical system) stipulates that this point of **Molad** represents the

Rebirth (*which I am referring to as Resurrection*) of the Moon. The **Molad** occurs *half way* through the Moons *Dark phase*, so this puts the time of the **Molad** (*Resurrection*) at *Early* Sunday morning, as stated in the New Testament of the bible.

Chapter Two - Light Verses Darkness, The Eternal Conflict

Analyzing the Symbolism of the Eternal Conflict between the Forces of Light and Darkness

The Never-Ending War Between The Vernal Equinox And The Autumnal Equinox

I'm certain that the most pervasive symbolism contained within the bible is the symbolism of the *never-ending* struggle between the forces of Light and Darkness. This is the central theme of much of the bible, and this symbolism is repeated over and over in various biblical Tales. This theme has been called the **Mono-Myth** by one great scholar (I believe Campbell), and that is certainly an excellent appellation. The *core* of the symbolical message contained in all of the allegories that describe the naturally alternating and blending forces of Light and Darkness is *Contention* - contention between right and wrong, free and enslaved, truth and falsehood, wealth and poverty. Sometimes this oscillation or strife (between the natural forces of light and darkness) is allegorically expressed as *war* between apposing kingdoms, or family conflicts, or some form of betrayal, degeneration or debasement. The

Ancients constructed their mythology to reflect the Personal and Political cycles of humanity. They even made geographical correlations between regions of the earth and the celestial domains.

The cycles of the vernal and autumnal equinoxes carry the greatest and most immediate impact on earthly life. Hence it is quite easy to understand that the importance and overwhelming relevance of the *equinoctial points* to Man's earthly environment generated a commensurate amount of attention and focus for the Writers of ancient mythology - a mythology that was designed to **record** the intervals and sequences of astronomical cycles and also to **preserve and update** mathematical formulas and calculations that were devised for the correct tracking of Time. The vernal equinox and the autumnal equinox (points due East and due West respectively) mark and designate the beginning of Spring and the beginning of Fall in it's turn. **This is of enormous importance**, because these celestial Indicators served to notify the Ancients *When* the *Time* had arrived to **Plant** and likewise *When* the *Time* had arrived to **Harvest.** These two Points (due East and due West) marked the birth of each day's Light (sun) as the sun rose above the eastern horizon and the death of the sun when it sunk below the western horizon.

The Sun crosses the vernal equinox on *March 21* and it crosses the autumnal equinox on *September 22*. These two dates are *186-187 days* apart. **Therefore when we seek out symbolism** that refers to the equinoctial cycles, we must look for these dates and/or intervals of time. **The bible is a Registry of Astronomical Phenomena written in a Mythological format**. The Sun and the Moon are the Primary Targets of most biblical Symbolism, i.e. the Tracking of their movements. These two celestial Bodies are the closest and most visible regulators of Time. **The Focus, Intention and Purpose** of the biblical Editors was to *Record and Preserve a System* for the Correct Tracking of Time cycles throughout succeeding human generations. Consequently, if and when we find a Personified **Symbol of the Sun** (Person, Kingdom, etc) tracing movements that correspond *In Time or Intervals of Time* to the aforementioned (equinoctial coordinates and the span of days between those points) – we then may be on the correct path to deciphering the pertinent biblical symbolism. Of course the Equinoxes are not the only points by which we may correlate biblical symbolism – but I am focusing on those celestial coordinates within this chapter, for the sake of clarity.

CELESTIAL CARDINAL POINTS

The following graphic depicts the cardinal points of the sun's ecliptic, that is the *apparent* path of the sun around the earth. **SS** is the *Summer Solstice* which defines the highest altitude of the sun in the course of a year at about Plus 23 ½ degrees. **WS** is the *Winter Solstice* which defines the lowest altitude of the sun in the course of a year at about Minus 23 ½ degrees. **AE** is the *Autumnal Equinox* at zero degrees declination – the sun at this point marks the beginning of Fall. **VE** is the *Vernal Equinox* at zero degrees declination – the sun at this point marks the beginning of Spring.

The ecliptic arc (VE SS AE) lies in the northern hemisphere above the celestial equator. The ecliptic arc (AE WS VE) lies in the southern hemisphere below the celestial equator.

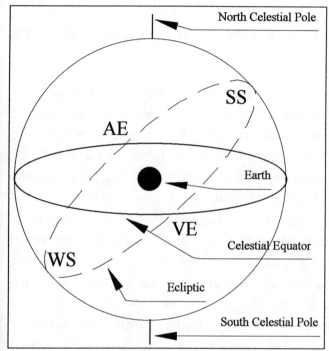

Figure 2: Celestial Equator and Sun's Ecliptic

ENSLAVEMENT OF THE ISRAELITES TO EGYPT IS PURE FABLE

A classical example of Equinoctial Symbolism is the story of the Israeli enslavement to Egypt. This Tale cannot be verified by any secular historical records. The whole account is a biblical myth. The biblical Israel is a symbol of the sun. As I have mentioned before, the Ancients used various celestial entities as Time Indicators, but the sun and moon are the major indicators for Time measurement. The Ancients tracked the movement of the sun and as the sun traversed various regions of the cosmos – this movement, of course, indicated the seasons of the year. But the Ancients recorded the sun's transits in an Allegorical format – they labeled the celestial regions with zodiacal names and they attached various symbolical *designations* to the sun. Sometimes these metaphorical names of the sun were personal and renowned and at other times political or community names.

The Egyptian-Hebrew saga is an instance where the Ancients signified the sun as a community i.e. Israel. Not only is the overall Tale of the Hebrew enslavement a symbolism of the transits of the sun, but also the *component parts of the fable are repetitions* of the same symbolical theme. The entire Saga of the Israeli Family from it's beginning with Abraham onward through the succeeding Patriarchs to it's conclusion is a continuous Repetition of the Same theme – that is a symbolism of the *natural contention* between the cosmic forces of the northern hemisphere and southern hemisphere. These two celestial regions (northern and southern hemispheres) are divided by the celestial equator. The point where the sun's ecliptic crosses the celestial equator defines the equinoxes. The equinoxes are the doors that our sun must pass through to inter and exit each region. The sun's crossing of the equinoxes is, in a symbolical sense, the crossing of a national border – a point that defines the separations of powers. And throughout the scriptures the Ancients have symbolically referred to these celestial coordinates as *contenders.*

Our task within this chapter is to exemplify chronological correspondences that prove and clarify astronomical symbolisms that allegorically depict the *equinoctial points* and the two apposing celestial regions i.e. the *northern and southern hemispheres.* Before we proceed in establishing the chronological proofs of my assertions, let's review a portion of *The Astrological Foundation Of The Christ Myth, Book Two* that addresses this issue of Hebrew symbolism:

"In the original astronomical mythology, the Chosen people symbolized the Sun, while traversing the region above the equinoxes. Also, that summer region above the equinoxes was symbolized as the promised land, the land of Israel (the chosen). The Winter region

below the equinoxes was symbolized as Egypt. This underworld region was where the Sun(Chosen) was enslaved and persecuted. The Underworld was the region of the Egyptians(Gentiles), those who opposed and persecuted Gods Chosen(the Sun). The Sun lost much of it's light and power in the underworld region. The ancients visualized the Sun(Chosen) as losing God's Favor, while in that region of trials and persecution. But, the net result of the Chastening effect of the nether world was to renew the Sun(the Chosen). The Faith and Devotion of the Sun(Chosen) was regenerated by the punitive elements of the nether world(underworld)."..........

*"Both allegories i.e. the biblical histories of Israel as well as Jesus Christ, symbolize the annual Life Cycle of the Solar Sun. **This mythology is derived** from the ancient religious, astronomical, symbolism of Egypt - a mythology(religion) based and formulated on the Cycles of the Sun, Moon, Stars and planets within the Cosmos. The period of the Sun below the equinoxes(Fall - winter), when it's heat and light became weakened, was represented by the ancients, as Persecution, Enslavement, Tribulation, Torment and finally Death. The **Resurgence of the Sun** at the vernal equinox (Spring - Summer) was symbolized as Resurrection, Victory, Freedom, Favorable Judgment, Salvation and/ or the Promised Land"*

As we proceed with our biblical decipherment, *it is important to note this aspect* – the *designations* of biblical symbolism are not rigid, but tend to blend. **In other words,** even though Israel is a symbol of the sun, when Israel (the sun) is at the vernal equinox it may take on the characteristics of the equinox and through association become (blend into) a symbol of the same – and likewise when in the area above the equinoxes, be equated to that region. The same holds true with Egypt, as a symbol of the autumnal equinox – Egypt also symbolized the entire space below the equinoxes, i.e. the region of Israel's (the suns') captivity.

CHRONOLOGY OF ISRAELS SYMBOLIC ENSLAVEMENT TO EGYPT:

Deuteronomy 16

[1]Observe the month of __Abib__, and keep the __passover__ unto the LORD thy God: **for in the month of Abib the LORD thy God brought thee forth out of Egypt by night.** *[2]Thou shalt therefore sacrifice the __passover__ unto the LORD thy God, of the flock and the herd, in the place which the LORD shall choose to place his name there. [3]Thou shalt eat no leavened bread with it; seven days shalt thou eat unleavened bread therewith, even the bread of affliction; for thou camest forth out of the land of Egypt in haste: that thou mayest remember the day when thou camest forth out of the land of Egypt all the days of thy life.*

Numbers 33

[1]These are the journeys of the children of Israel, which went forth out of the land of Egypt with their armies under the hand of Moses and Aaron. [2]And Moses wrote their goings out according to their journeys by the commandment of the LORD: and these are their journeys according to their goings out. [3]And **they departed from Rameses in the first month, on the fifteenth day of the first month; on the morrow after the** __**passover**__ *the children of Israel went out with an high hand in the sight of all the Egyptians.*

Both of these biblical verses describe the Journeys of Israel, and we know of course, that Israel is symbolic of the sun. Furthermore both of these verses depict Israel in association with Egypt. We also know, that according to our decipherment of biblical allegory, Egypt is symbolic of the celestial region that lies beneath the equinoxes - also known as the southern hemisphere (that section of Space with Declinations below the Celestial Equator). **The focus** of each of these verses is the **timeframe** of the Israeli **departure** from Egypt. The actual sun's departure from the southern hemisphere is marked by it's crossing of the vernal equinox.

So our task is fairly simple – we need only establish a chronological correlation between the *biblical journey* of **Israel out of Egypt** and the *celestial journey* of the **sun** *out of the Southern Hemisphere*. And once we have established this correlation, we will have provided another leg of support for my assertions in regards to biblical allegory - that shows Israel symbolical of the sun and Egypt as a symbol of the southern hemisphere.

The biblical verses noted above convey some indications of the timeframe of the Hebrew's exodus – **we are told directly** in the verse from *Deuteronomy* that their exit was made in the month[15] of *Abib*. **The verse** from *Numbers* gives us the date as

---

[15] These are Jewish months based on the Jewish calendar. See Appendix for calendar information

the *First month and the fifteenth day* **and** **both** verses stipulate a *Binding* connection to the *Passover* observance.

The term *Abib* stands for the month called Nisan[16]. *Abib* was the name for the first month of the Jewish religious year prior to their adopting the name *Nisan* for that month - the term Nisan is of Babylonian origin. So according to the bible the Hebrews exited from Egypt under the *Full Moon* (15th day) in the month of *Nisan*. Furthermore, according to the bible, the commemoration of this event **must for all times** be connected to the **Passover** observance.

And we all know that the Passover observance is the Full Moon of the First month of the Jewish *religious* year after the sun crosses the Vernal Equinox.

There is no questioning the fact that the exodus of the Hebrews from Egypt correlates to the sun's crossing the vernal equinox. And the biblical injunction just read clearly stipulates that this connection between the Hebrew exodus and the suns crossing of the vernal equinox must never be forgotten – hence the yearly Passover observance as a reminder.

---

[16] Nisan is the 1st month of the Jewish religious year as stipulated in Exodus 12. Tishri is the 1st month of the Jewish calendar year.

So the correlation between the Hebrew Exodus and the sun crossing the vernal equinox *is absolute and certain.* **The Key point to remember is this** - since it is abundantly clear that there never was a Hebrew nation that was in bondage to Egypt historically, and likewise the fanciful tale of the Exodus never took place in history - *it follows as a matter of basic logic* that the clear correlation between the *exit of the Hebrews* from Egypt and the *exit of the sun* from the Southern Hemisphere must represent astronomical symbolism, or nothing at all. **There is no reason** for the astronomical association of the sun with Israel to exist relative to an exodus, except as symbolism – that is unless you *choose* to believe that the biblical myth (of an exodus) is historical.

RESURRECTION OF JESUS CORELLATES TO THE SUN'S CROSSING THE VERNAL EQUINOX

From Dictionary.com

easter originally a Saxon word (Eostre), denoting a goddess of the Saxons, in honour of whom sacrifices were offered about the time of the Passover. Hence the name came to be given to the festival of the Resurrection of Christ, which occured at the time of the Passover. In the early English versions this word was frequently used as the translation of the Greek pascha (the Passover). When the Authorized Version (1611) was formed, the word "passover" was used in all passages in which this word pascha occurred, except in Act 12:4. In the Revised Version the proper word, "passover," is always used.

<u>Source</u>: *Easton's 1897 Bible Dictionary*

John 19:12-19

[12] And from thenceforth Pilate sought to release him: but the Jews cried out, saying, If thou let this man go, thou art not Caesar's friend: whosoever maketh himself a king speaketh against Caesar. [13] When Pilate therefore heard that saying, he brought Jesus forth, and sat down in the judgment seat in a place that is called the Pavement, but in the Hebrew, Gabbatha. [14] And it was the preparation of the <u>passover</u>, and about the sixth hour: and he saith unto the Jews, Behold your King! [15] But they cried out, Away with him, away with him, crucify him. Pilate saith unto them, Shall I crucify your King? The chief priests answered, We have no king but Caesar.

[16] Then delivered he him therefore unto them to be crucified. And they took Jesus, and led him away. [17] And he bearing his cross went forth into a place called the place of a skull, which is called in the Hebrew Golgotha: [18] Where they crucified him, and two other with him, on either side one, and Jesus in the midst.

Underlining is my own

We can see from the two insertions above that the resurrection of Jesus was tied to the Passover and hence to the sun's crossing of the vernal equinox. This is not coincidental – both Jesus and Israel are Symbols of the sun and their suffering, captivity and eventual liberation (into the upper regions) are in parallel.

JESUS SYMBOLIZED THE VERNAL EQUINOX AND JOHN THE BAPTIST SYMBOLIZED THE AUTUMNAL EQUINOX

Often the symbolism of the equinoxes comes in the type of *twins* or *cousins* or *male contenders*. At times the sun's crossing the equinox is viewed as a *marriage* of the sun with its bride (the vernal equinox). Of course, the suns crossing of the vernal equinox also symbolizes *impregnation* and sometimes *debasement*, *forfeiture* or *seduction* at the autumnal equinox. The war of the equinoxes is Light against Darkness – and this conflict generates points of demarcation that enable us to measure Time.

However it is interesting to note, that in the case of Jesus Christ (the vernal equinox) and John The Baptist (the autumnal equinox) – the relinquishing of power was *not* challenged but, on the contrary, John seemed eager to transfer the mantle of leadership to his cousin, Jesus. Let's explore the relationship between these two mythical characters, Jesus Christ and John The Baptist – to determine their fit as symbolical representatives of the equinoxes.

First, take a careful read of the following biblical verses

Luke 1:26 through Luke 1:44

[26] *And in the* **sixth month** *the angel Gabriel was sent from God unto a city of Galilee, named Nazareth,* [27] *To a virgin espoused to a man whose name was Joseph, of the house of David; and the virgin's name was Mary.* [28] *And the angel came in unto her, and said, Hail, thou that art highly favoured, the Lord is with thee: blessed art thou among women.* [29] *And when she saw him, she was troubled at his saying, and cast in her mind what manner of salutation this should be.* [30] *And the angel said unto her, Fear not, Mary: for thou hast found favour with God.* [31] *And, behold,* **thou shalt conceive in thy womb, and bring forth a son, and shalt call his name JESUS.** [32] *He shall be great, and shall be called the Son of the Highest: and the Lord God shall give unto him the throne of his father David:* [33] *And he shall reign over the house of Jacob for ever; and of his kingdom there shall be no end.* [34] *Then said Mary unto the angel, How shall this be, seeing I know not a man?* [35] *And the angel answered and said unto her, The Holy Ghost shall come upon thee, and the power of the Highest shall overshadow thee: therefore also that holy thing which shall be born of thee shall be called the Son of God.* [36] ***And, behold, thy cousin Elisabeth, she hath also conceived a son in her old age: and this is the sixth month with her,*** *who was called barren.* [37] *For with God nothing shall be impossible.* [38] *And Mary said, Behold the handmaid of the Lord; be it unto me according to thy word. And the angel departed from her.*

[39] *And Mary arose in those days, and went into the hill country with haste, into a city of Juda;* [40] *And entered into the house of Zacharias, and saluted Elisabeth.* [41] *And it came to pass, that, when Elisabeth heard the salutation of Mary, the babe leaped in her womb; and Elisabeth was filled with the Holy Ghost:* [42] *And she spake out with a loud voice, and said, Blessed art thou among women, and blessed is the fruit of thy womb.* [43] *And whence is*

this to me, that the mother of my Lord should come to me? ⁴⁴*For, lo, as soon as the voice of thy salutation sounded in mine ears, the babe leaped in my womb for joy.*

Luke 1:56 through Luke 1:64

⁵⁶**And Mary abode with her about three months, and returned to her own house.**⁵⁷**Now Elisabeth's full time came that she should be delivered; and she brought forth a son.** ⁵⁸*And her neighbours and her cousins heard how the Lord had showed great mercy upon her; and they rejoiced with her.* ⁵⁹*And it came to pass, that on the eighth day they came to circumcise the child; and they called him Zacharias, after the name of his father.* ⁶⁰*And his mother answered and said, Not so; but* **he shall be called John.** ⁶¹*And they said unto her, There is none of thy kindred that is called by this name.* ⁶²*And they made signs to his father, how he would have him called.* ⁶³*And he asked for a writing table, and wrote, saying, His name is John. And they marvelled all.* ⁶⁴*And his mouth was opened immediately, and his tongue loosed, and he spake, and praised God.*

Our first step in analyzing these verses will be the identification of the characters – We have *Mary,* the mother of the expected savior *Jesus,* and her husband *Joseph,* the angel *Gabriel* who brings the message to Mary as to what is in store for her as the appointed mother of God. We have *Elisabeth,* Mary's cousin and the mother of *John* The Baptist, also present is *Zacharias* – the father of John The Baptist.

The integrity of the symbolism is well maintained within these verses. Jesus and John are not twin brothers, but as the sons

of cousins they hold identical relationships and this is fine –
they are on the same *Level* in terms of their genealogy, which
matches the equinoxes which are on the same *Level* in terms of
declination. The biblical editors have supplied us with the
necessary math that will enable us to define the *symbolical
identities* of the major subjects i.e. Jesus and John.

We are told in Luke 1:26 that the *angel came to Mary in the 6th
month of the Jewish calendar.* In verses 27 and 31 we are informed
that Mary is still a virgin and that she is not yet pregnant – and
further that she has been appointed mother of the expected
Son of God, and her **impregnation is imminent**. We are
told in verse 36 that *Elizabeth is in her 6th month* (actually
completed 6 months) of pregnancy and this, of course, means
that Elizabeth was impregnated in the 1st month (the autumnal
equinox) – **we know this** because the Editors have already
noted (in Luke 1:26) that this meeting between Mary and the
Angel took place in the 6th month of the Jewish calendar[17]. So
with *6 months between the impregnation of Elizabeth and her cousin
Mary* – this means that *Mary was impregnated in the 7th*[18] *month* of
the Jewish calendar (the vernal equinox).

---

[17] See Appendix for information on the Jewish calendar

[18] Mary's Immaculate Conception was signaled by the angel Gabriel as Imminent

Verses 39, 40, 56, 57 tell us that Mary visited her cousin Elisabeth and stayed with her for 3 months till *John The Baptist* was born. In the second chapter of Luke, the birth of the mythical Jesus is described.

The Scholars set the birth of *John The Baptist* as June 24. **This is correct**, because this date is **three days after the Summer Solstice**. *John's* conception was at the **Autumnal Equinox** and his birth was near the Summer Solstice. The sequence of John's conception and birth is a mirrored reflection of the Christ (his conception and birth). *John* was the *Twin* cousin of *Jesus*. The *Christ* was conceived at the **Vernal Equinox** and was born **three days after the Winter Solstice** on December 25. Christ was the son of Spirit, John was the son of Matter.

The fact the Mary was impregnated at the time of the vernal equinox fits into esoteric symbolism as I explained in Book Two, **See Quote:** *The Astrological Foundation Of The Christ Myth, Book Two* Page 32,

"The astronomical explanation of the first three points is as follows, **The Miraculous Conception**, *as I explained in the previous chapter, refers to the* **Conjugation(Conception)** *that annually takes place at the vernal equinox. God, the Father, the Sun personified, at this time ((of) the vernal equinox) is joined(the crossing of the celestial equator and the ecliptic of the sun) to commence the Gestation of the Son (Sun) of God(Father Sun), that will be born 280 days later on December 25th"*

I will interject here that the Hebrews use a Lunar calendar and since Lunar time cycles are not in natural sync with solar time cycles, the Lunar calendar must be periodically adjusted through methods of intercalation. In consequence of this and various astronomical factors, the first day of their year Tishri 1 may not occur exactly at the autumnal equinox and the first day of their 7th month Nisan 1 may not occur exactly at the vernal equinox. This is not important, because both the 1st and 7th month of the Hebrew calendar are pegged to the equinoxes - this is verified by the festivals of **Yom Kippur** and **Passover**. So the fact that the Jewish *New Year lunar date* (which occurs proximate to the equinox crossing) may shift a *little*, relative to solar date of the equinox, means absolutely nothing as far as it relates to this biblical symbolism.

In **John** of the bible the biblical Editors give a Bold hint as to the symbolical identity of Jesus and John.
Read the Following:

John 3:26 through John 3:31

^{26}*And they came unto John, and said unto him, Rabbi, he that was with thee beyond Jordan, to whom thou barest witness, behold, the same baptizeth, and all men come to him.*
^{27}*John answered and said, A man can receive nothing, except it be given him from heaven.*
^{28}*Ye yourselves bear me witness, that I said, I am not the Christ, but that I am sent before him.* ^{29}*He that hath the bride is the bridegroom: but the friend of the bridegroom, which*

standeth and heareth him, rejoiceth greatly because of the bridegroom's voice: this my joy therefore is fulfilled. **³⁰He must increase, but I must decrease.** *³¹He that cometh from above is above all: he that is of the earth is earthly, and speaketh of the earth: he that cometh from heaven is above all.*

The phrase spoken by the mythical *John* – **"He must increase, but I must decrease"** – goes to the *core* of the astronomical functions of the equinoxes. The equinoxes are the astronomical points that define the proportions of daily sunlight and darkness on our planet. The span of daytime and nighttime are at equilibrium when the sun is at the declination of the equinoxes, but the *increased* daytime caused by the suns ascension into the region above the equinoxes (northern hemisphere) must, by the natural law of physics, bring *decrease* to the effects of the autumnal equinox. This is Vivid!

Trace the name John to the Latin and we find the term *Ioannes* – *Ioannes* was an ancient deity that was half fish and half man. *Ioannes* is the counterpart of the Philistine god, *Dagon.* As we know, the Philistines represented the autumnal equinox in the Old Testament as *opponents* of Israel, which symbolized the vernal equinox. So it is interesting to note that the Editors of the New Testament have maintained the integrity of the symbolism by this obvious link between *John The Baptist* and the *Philistines* – both as symbols of the autumnal equinox and both as images/subjects of Dagon/Ioannes.

In summary - within this chapter, we have related to the environmental influences of the sun as it annually alternates between the northern hemisphere and the southern hemisphere. These spheres are divided by the celestial equator. The climatic conditions on earth are reversed in accordance with the sun's position, north or south of the celestial equator.

We have shown that the Ancients symbolized these two Divisions of space as apposing Kingdoms or Powers. And furthermore, they symbolized the sun as giving power to whatever section it occupied, or being held captive by that region or in obeisance to that region. We have shown that the equinoxes are the Gateways between the regions (Kingdoms) and are symbolized as such. **To this day**, both Israel and Jesus are looked upon as Gateways to God's Kingdom.

In the case of Israel and the Egyptians, the two hemispheres were symbolized as hostile combatants (master and slave). In the case of Jesus and John, the regions were allegorically depicted as transitional (spiritual) powers.

Our Primary focus is on the Perpetual *Dualism* denoted between these *astronomical Forces* (regions), north and south – that the Ancients depicted in their **Religious Parallels** as

Dualistic Spiritual Forces. We have now formed a basis for entrance into our next chapter.

Chapter Three - The Duality Of The God Concept

Exploring the Astronomical Foundation of Atonement and Sacrificial Rites

At the core of Christian theology is the concept of the Fall of Mankind from God's grace and the need for humanity to Atone for their sins - and further that the Agent or Intercessor through whom expiation must be attained is Jesus Christ. Of course the Atonement aspect is present in all religions, that is to say the perceived need for God's forgiveness and the *willingness* of the believers to subject themselves to *self-affliction* as a proof of their sincerity.

The literal application of the sacrificial tenets of religion is perhaps the most abhorrent and unfortunate result of misguided faith. History reveals that mindless bloodletting and gross mutilations have been conducted by the faithful on every continent and in every era of human history. The book "The Golden Bough" is an excellent Read for information on this subject. **This asinine conception**, that a worthy god could be bloodthirsty, vengeful, and jealous**, is directly connected to the symbolism** that reflects the natural contention between the **apposing hemispheres**. This attitude (that the anger of god must be appeased through blood sacrifice) remains at the core of religious philosophy to this day, even though refined and intellectualized.

The Christian concept of religious sacrifice or penitence is a duplication of the Jewish concept. The theological basis for both is identical. And both Christian and Jewish atonement precepts are symbolizations of the suns seemingly uncertain status[19] when transiting from one hemisphere to the other. Physics teaches us that all movement creates friction and that changes in the direction and/or rate of movement creates greater friction. **In other words**, in order for the sun to cross from one Polarity into the Realm of another Polarity, it must conquer a point of *Natural Inflection*, and *increased resistance* at the focal point and environs of that locality of transition (equinoxes). All of the rites of penitence practiced at the time of Passover, Easter and Yom Kippur, such as fasting, congregational prayer, chanting, and even the sacrificial bloodletting of old tend to impose on the religious aspirant trials and test that parallel the cosmic struggles of the sun.

In addition to this, when the sun is successful in making it's transit of either equinox into the zone of the other

---

[19] Of course the climatic uncertainty is experienced on earth, not the sun – but the sun is the focus of the symbolism.

hemisphere – the natural cosmic forces of the sun are blended with the hemisphere in which it dwells. The Ancients, in some instances portrayed this transition (symbolically and biblically) as the sun's (Israel's) *defection or desertion* from one King in favor of another King. The sun, in a symbolical sense had switched loyalties i.e. committed treason. This point of fact leads to an understanding of the symbolism related to *sacrificial rites* – the price that the ungrateful and fickle sun (Israel) had to pay when it made the inevitable return into the hemisphere (godly domain) that it had previously deserted. I shall, in due course, supply biblical verses that support my contentions, but first witness these quotes from *Book Two* which help to explain how the Ancients formulated their religious tenets in reflection of astronomical phenomena.

From Chapter 7 of Book Two

"The original astronomical(mythological) data base dealt with the eternally conflicting forces of Darkness/netherworld(southern hemisphere) and the forces of Light/ Paradise(northern hemisphere). Physical Nature is not capable of distinguishing morality or immorality, right or wrong, good or bad. Nature is Driven by the Laws of Instinct, Gravity, Energy and Matter, and it's interactions. No morality is involved here. The universe is, without doubt, managed by natural law, which does not waver for any non-lawful reason.

***The Human Being**, in that He is part Matter(physical instinctive nature) and part spirit(Metaphysical nature), **is also**, like the opposing forces of universal nature, constantly* *at war(conflict)* **within Himself** *Religion tends to balance this eternal and internal moral conflict, within the Human species.*

The Evolution from astronomy to Religion *was done by adapting religious correlations* **to** *the opposing spheres(the region below the equinoxes verses the region above the equinoxes) of natural contention.* **The forces** *of the northern hemisphere , in their religious parallels, represented the positive spiritual natures. The Forces of the Southern Hemisphere represented the negative instinctive natures.* **The Never Ending War of the Sun(Light) to overcome or destroy darkness** *, <u>in it's Religious Parallels,</u> became the Never Ending Struggle of Man's Spiritual Nature to Dominate his Carnal(beastly) Nature."*

From Chapter 5 of Book Two

"The number forty represents pure symbolism and allegorically expresses the **interval of time** *between the sun reaching certain celestial coordinates(the equinoxes), and it's(sun's) tangible effect upon the climate of our planet, after reaching those coordinates.* **The interval is forty days,** *even though the biblical editors may use weeks, or years, or hours, in the text, according to the subject matter of the tale , so that the unit(description) used will fit the context of the specific fable.*

The interval is always referred to as a Struggle of some sort, some type of deprivation, or trial, or test. This is because of the extreme difficulty our solar sun experiences in vanquishing the winter cold from our atmosphere. After six months under the equator, the sun is now in position , when it reaches the vernal equinox on March 21, to restore warmth and moisture to the northern regions. But the victory of warmth over cold is not immediate, but rather a tug of war , back and forth, between the forces of light (warmth, salvation, reward and blessings) and darkness (cold, tempting devil, Satan).

But after 40 days (May Day), you can rest assured that the frost won't ruin your crops. The sun is now victorious, and free of the tempting(tugging) devil of winter......

This Forty refers to the Lag Time *between the Sun reaching the equinoxes, to the actual Terrestrial effect on the earth , that takes about 40 days to materialize. The Spring and the Fall begin officially when the Sun crosses the Equinoxes, but the effect on the earth's weather is delayed for a period of forty days".*

The Character Of God

Our task, at this juncture, is to clarify *Dualism* as a *God Concept,* by exemplifying the methodology of the Ancients in formulating their religious philosophy. They (Priesthood) have been faithful to the same system of esoteric symbolism throughout history i.e. *they have fashioned theology in exact parallel to natural and astronomical phenomena.* **They have created** a *God Concept* that is a direct reflection of the interactions within the material universe. **The Positive and Negative polarities of matter have been symbolized theologically as contending spiritual forces.**

When this theology is accurately perceived, the devil does not represent the popularly accepted concept of sin (lying, adultery, murder, stealing etc.), but rather the devil denotes opposition, challenge, contention and/or friction. This is the biblical message that we shall explore. Without a doubt, the bible contains some laudable moral and social precepts but also, without doubt, the worst purveyors of corruption and sin have been god's disciples.

Read the bible – we find that Cain murdered his brother, Lot prostituted his daughters and on another occasion had sex with his daughters– *Genesis 19:6-8, Genesis 19:30-38*, Noah could be classified as a drunkard *Genesis 9:20-23*, Abraham prostituted his wife – *Genesis 20:1-13*, Jacob (Israel) was a thief and a Con artist – *Genesis 25:29-34, Genesis 27:1-29*, Moses was a murderer and fugitive *Exodus 2:11-15*, David was an adulterer and a murderer *2 Samuel 11:2-17* and there are many more examples of atrocities and/or sins committed by god's disciples. The point being – morality does not hold the highest priority with the god of the bible.

Indeed, the biblical god is extremely jealous – he demands fear, worship, praise and *blood* sacrifice and will viciously torture and slaughter those that fail to hail him as the only and greatest of gods. Let's explore a few biblical verses that describe the character of the biblical god – **take special note** that the biblical god's *persistent theme* throughout these verses is *self-centered* monotheism, not morality. He demands complete devotion and threatens us with dire consequences if we reject him.

Exodus 20:1 through Exodus 20:5

¹*And God spake all these words, saying,* ²*I am the* LORD *thy God, which have brought thee out of the land of Egypt, out of the house of bondage.* ³**Thou shalt have no other gods before me.** ⁴*Thou shalt not make unto thee any graven image, or any likeness of any thing that is in heaven above, or that is in the earth beneath, or that is in the water under the earth:* ⁵*Thou shalt not bow down thyself to them, nor serve them: for* **I the** LORD **thy God am a jealous God,** *visiting the iniquity of the fathers upon the children unto the third and fourth generation of them that hate me;*

Exodus 34:13 through Exodus 34:16

¹³*But ye shall destroy their altars, break their images, and cut down their groves:* ¹⁴**For thou shalt worship no other god:** *for the* LORD, *whose name is Jealous, is a jealous God:* ¹⁵*Lest thou make a covenant with the inhabitants of the land, and they go a whoring after their gods, and do sacrifice unto their gods, and one call thee, and thou eat of his sacrifice;* ¹⁶*And thou take of their daughters unto thy sons, and their daughters go a whoring after their gods, and make thy sons go a whoring after their gods.*

Joshua 24:19 through Joshua 24:20

¹⁹*And Joshua said unto the people, Ye cannot serve the* LORD: *for he is an holy God;* **he is a jealous God;** *he will not forgive your transgressions nor your sins.* ²⁰**If ye forsake the** LORD, **and serve strange gods, then he will turn and do you hurt, and consume you,** *after that he hath done you good.*

Judges 10:10

*[10]And the children of Israel cried unto the LORD, saying, We have **sinned** against thee, both **because we have forsaken our God**, and also served Baalim.*

Judges 10:13

*[13]Yet ye have forsaken me, **and served other gods**: wherefore I will deliver you no more.*

Exodus 23:31 through Exodus 23:33

*[31]And I will set thy bounds from the Red sea even unto the sea of the Philistines, and from the desert unto the river: for I will deliver the inhabitants of the land into your hand; and thou shalt drive them out before thee. [32]**Thou shalt make no covenant with them, nor with their gods**. [33]They shall not dwell in thy land, lest they make thee sin against me: **for if thou serve their gods**, it will surely be a snare unto thee.*

The viciousness in the following verses is astounding and the bible is full of this type of content

Leviticus 26:1 through Leviticus 26:2

[1]Ye shall make you no idols nor graven image, neither rear you up a standing image, neither shall ye set up any image of stone in your land, to bow down unto it: for I am the LORD your God. [2]Ye shall keep my sabbaths, and reverence my sanctuary: I am the LORD.

Leviticus 26:14 through Leviticus 26:17

[14]But if ye will not hearken unto me, and will not do all these commandments; [15]And if ye shall despise my statutes, or if your soul abhor my judgments, so that ye will not do all my commandments, but that ye break my covenant: [16]I also will do this unto you; I will even appoint over you terror, consumption, and the burning ague, that shall consume the eyes, and cause sorrow of heart: and ye shall sow your seed in vain, for your enemies shall eat it. [17]And I will set my face against you, and ye shall be slain before your enemies: they that hate you shall reign over you; and ye shall flee when none pursueth you.

Leviticus 26:21 through Leviticus 26:22

[21]And if ye walk contrary unto me, and will not hearken unto me; I will bring seven times more plagues upon you according to your sins. [22]I will also send wild beasts among you, which shall rob you of your children, and destroy your cattle, and make you few in number; and your high ways shall be desolate.

Leviticus 26:25

[25]And I will bring a sword upon you, that shall avenge the quarrel of my covenant: and when ye are gathered together within your cities, I will send the pestilence among you; and ye shall be delivered into the hand of the enemy.

Leviticus 26:29 through Leviticus 26:33

[29]And ye shall eat the flesh of your sons, and the flesh of your daughters shall ye eat. [30]And I will destroy your high places, and cut down your images, and cast your carcases upon the carcases of your idols, and my soul shall abhor you. [31]And I will

make your cities waste, and bring your sanctuaries unto desolation, and I will not smell the savour of your sweet odours. [32] And I will bring the land into desolation: and your enemies which dwell therein shall be astonished at it. [33] And I will scatter you among the heathen, and will draw out a sword after you: and your land shall be desolate, and your cities waste.

I have inserted these numerous verses into our text, because an accurate understanding of the *character and personality* of the biblical god is **central** to interpreting the esoteric symbolism as it pertains to Atonement and Sacrificial rites. It is very difficult to find examples of the highly touted god (of heavenly character) within the bible – that is the loving, compassionate, generous and benevolent lord of salvation that we all have heard so much about. Even Jesus Christ had his bad days – witness this verse:

Luke 14:25 through Luke 14:26

[25] *And there went great multitudes with him: and he turned, and said unto them,* [26] *If any man come to me, and hate not his father, and mother, and wife, and children, and brethren, and sisters, yea, and his own life also, he cannot be my disciple.*

There can be no doubt after reading the verses above as to the character of our biblical god – he is extremely Combative, and capable of heinous cruelty toward those that fail to worship him with complete devotion. The biblical god is a contentious god, obsessed with *one* overwhelming compulsion – that is the complete control and devotion of his subjects (Israel which symbolizes the sun). But (Israel) the sun is fickle and torn between two gods - and the other god at the opposite Hemisphere is no less demanding. The God at the Northern Hemisphere (polarity) represents the positive, male attributes and the God at the Southern Hemisphere (polarity) represents the negative, female attributes – this is the *Solar* symbolism. The natural fate of the sun (biblical Israel) is to spend eternity oscillating between the forces of positive and negative polarities. The Summer Solstice (sign of Cancer) is the Seat of the Higher God and the Winter Solstice (sign of Capricorn) is the Seat of the Lower God (Devil). The term Devil, within the symbolism, does not indicate evil, but rather opposition and contention.

Let us examine the biblical injunctions in regards to Atonement and Sacrifice and do our best to clarify the Astronomical and Religious linkage between the two. We will follow the same methodology as in the previous chapters – that is we shall exemplify a *chronological correspondence* between the actions of the biblical symbol vis-à-vis the actual solar sun - also we will provide an explanation of the astronomical symbolism.

ATONEMENT AND SACRIFICIAL RITES

The Date of the Observance

Leviticus 16:29 through Leviticus 16:34

[29] And this shall be a statute for ever unto you: that in the seventh month, on the tenth day of the month, ye shall afflict your souls, and do no work at all, whether it be one of your own country, or a stranger that sojourneth among you: [30] For on that day shall the priest make an atonement for you, to cleanse you, that ye may be clean from all your sins before the LORD. [31] It shall be a sabbath of rest unto you, and ye shall afflict your souls, by a statute for ever. [32] And the priest, whom he shall anoint, and whom he shall consecrate to minister in the priest's office in his father's stead, shall make the atonement, and shall put on the linen clothes, even the holy garments: [33] And he shall make an atonement for the holy sanctuary, and he shall make an atonement for the tabernacle of the congregation, and for the altar, and he shall make an atonement for the priests, and for all the people of the congregation. [34] And this shall be an everlasting statute unto you, to make an atonement for the children of Israel for all their sins once a year. And he did as the LORD commanded Moses.

Description of the Ritual

Leviticus 16:7 through Leviticus 16:10

[7]And he shall take the two goats, and present them before the LORD at the door of the tabernacle of the congregation. [8]And Aaron shall cast lots upon the two goats; one lot for the LORD, and the other lot for the scapegoat. [9]And Aaron shall bring the goat upon which the LORD'S lot fell, and offer him for a sin offering. [10]But the goat, on which the lot fell to be the scapegoat, shall be presented alive before the LORD, to make an atonement with him, and to let him go for a scapegoat into the wilderness.

Leviticus 16:15 through Leviticus 16:17

[15]Then shall he kill the goat of the sin offering, that is for the people, and bring his blood within the veil, and do with that blood as he did with the blood of the bullock, and sprinkle it upon the mercy seat, and before the mercy seat: [16]And he shall make an atonement for the holy place, because of the uncleanness of the children of Israel, and because of their transgressions in all their sins: and so shall he do for the tabernacle of the congregation, that remaineth among them in the midst of their uncleanness. [17]And there shall be no man in the tabernacle of the congregation when he goeth in to make an atonement in the holy place,

until he come out, and have made an atonement for himself, and for his household, and for all the congregation of Israel.

Leviticus 16:20 through Leviticus 16:22

²⁰And when he hath made an end of reconciling the holy place, and the tabernacle of the congregation, and the altar, he shall bring the live goat: ²¹And Aaron shall lay both his hands upon the head of the live goat, and confess over him all the iniquities of the children of Israel, and all their transgressions in all their sins, putting them upon the head of the goat, and shall send him away by the hand of a fit man into the wilderness: ²²And the goat shall bear upon him all their iniquities unto a land not inhabited: and he shall let go the goat in the wilderness.

Also take note of this Definition of a Mythical creature from dictionary.com

azazel (Lev. 16:8, 10, 26, Revised Version only here; rendered "scape-goat" in the Authorized Version). This word has given rise to many different views. Some Jewish interpreters regard it as the name of a place some 12 miles east of Jerusalem, in the wilderness. Others take it to be the name of an evil spirit, or even of Satan. But when we remember that the two goats together form a type of Christ, on whom the Lord "laid the iniquity of us all," and examine into the root meaning of this word (viz., "separation"), the interpretation of those who regard the one goat as representing the atonement made, and the other, that "for Azazel," as representing the effect of the great work of atonement (viz., the complete removal of sin), is certainly to be preferred. The one goat which was "for Jehovah" was offered as a sin-offering, by which atonement was made. But the sins must also be visibly banished, and therefore they were symbolically laid by confession on the other goat, which was then "sent away for Azazel" into the wilderness. The form of this word indicates intensity, and therefore signifies the total separation of sin: it was wholly carried away. It was important that the result of the sacrifices offered by the high priest alone in the sanctuary should be embodied in a visible transaction, and hence the dismissal of the "scape-goat." It was of no consequence what became of it, as the whole import of the transaction lay in its being sent into the wilderness bearing away sin. As the goat "for Jehovah" was to witness to the demerit of sin and the need of the blood of atonement, so the goat "for Azazel" was to witness to the efficacy of the sacrifice and the result of the shedding of blood in the taking away of sin.

Source: *Easton's 1897 Bible Dictionary*

The insertions above, that follow the Heading, *Atonement and Sacrificial Rites* provide us with sufficient information to prove a seminal association between astronomy and the religious rites of Sacrificial Atonement, as practiced under Judaism and Christianity[20]. **Remember our Premise** – that the Ancients (Priesthood) created a *God Concept and theology* that is a mirrored reflection of the Material Universe. Our spiritual concepts are, in reality, humanly created symbolisms of

---

[20] The only reason we are focused on Judaism and Christianity is because the bible (the book of Jews and Christians) is the best ancient theological reference available to us of the English speaking world; but the astronomical religious connection applies to All religions of ancient origin.

---

natural and astronomical phenomena – Spirits based on Physics.

The line of demarcation between the apposing spheres of the universe as referenced from earth is the *celestial equator.* The *regulator of Time* as defined by it's duration within the domains of a particular hemisphere is the *sun.* The Gateways between the hemispheres are defined as the *equinoctial points* and the equinoctial points are designated as the *intersections* of the sun's ecliptic with the celestial equator. The sun crosses the equinoxes in the 1st and 7th months of the Jewish calendar. The chronology of the bible is based on the Jewish calendar. **The 1st month of the Jewish civil year** is *Tishri* which occurs near the autumnal equinox in the Fall of the year, but **the 1st month of the Jewish religious year** is *Nisan,* which occurs near the vernal equinox in the Spring of the year. Both, the religious or the civil year may be used in biblical symbolism. **Our focus,** at this point, is to show that the *Atonement tradition* is actually performed in recognition of a *Dualistic God Concept* that was fashioned in *imitation* of the dualism existent between the apposing northern and southern hemispheres.

With the aforementioned clarifications in mind, we may now begin our decipherment of the biblical verses from Leviticus that describe the Sacrificial Atonement. Of course, our task is to present reasonable evidence that these religious ceremonies are, in fact, *symbolical duplications of astronomical phenomena.*

Leviticus 16:29-34 stipulates that the Atonement must be on the 10ᵗʰ day of the 7ᵗʰ month. This is the month of Tishri that occurs after the autumnal equinox. We know that the autumnal equinox indicates the fall of the sun from positive to negative polarity. Symbolically, Israel is the sun - so the crossing of the autumnal equinox, in terms of the allegory, signifies captivity, defection, or transgression. According to the biblical verses that we are studying, the purpose of atonement is to earn forgiveness for ones transgressions through self-affliction and blood sacrifice. We know, as I have stated before, that the equinoxes allegorically represent the Gateways between apposing jurisdictions.

I must interject here with a mathematical definition of atonement. Check any good dictionary and you will find that the definition is *to reconcile*. **Mathematically,** *reconcile* means to reduce the difference between positive and negative numbers to zero. Both equinoxes perform this task of reconciliation, in that the suns declination is zero at the equinoctial points. In this symbolical mythological sense, the equinoxes are points of Judgment or a time to be judged or graded, if you will. This level of equilibrium and balance (zero degrees at the equinox) is a symbolical inference to Judgment, a period of Testing that determines what consequences may befall the Subject. **The Souls of the Aspirants are weighed on the Scales Of**

Judgment (at the equinox) is a symbolism that goes back to ancient Egypt and is *depicted on their Relief's*. Some smart Jews refer to the Day of Atonement as Judgment Day. *Jesus Christ* was referred to as the Mediator who ushers in Judgment – and this is accurate when we consider the cosmic action of the sun as a mediator (reconciles the differences between the hemispheres at the crossing of the equinoxes). Also, within the symbolism, the sun (Israel, Jesus) itself is being judged.

Leviticus 16:7-22 describes the Atonement ritual: The fact that Two Forces are being appeased by this ritual is indicated by the choice of two goats for the Sacrifice. The verses state that one *Lot* (label, Tag, luck of the draw, etc) is for the Lord and the other *Lot* is for the Scapegoat. This Scapegoat is dedicated to the *Goat*, zodiacal sign of Capricorn (the sign of the goat). Capricorn symbolizes the lower god, the devil, Azazel. The *labeled* Scapegoat is sent into the Wilderness. **Under biblical symbolism**, the terms *Wilderness* and *Desert* almost always refer to the hemisphere under the equinoxes – also the terms Pit, Grave, Hell, Cave, and others *may* indicate the southern sphere. **I included the dictionary definition** of the Wilderness Demon (Azazel) because I think the explicit Duality of the Atonement Sacrifice is well indicated in the definition. Azazel is Capricorn is the Devil. The other goat is slaughtered and it's blood sprinkled about the Sanctuary as a Sin Offering. We are told in verses 20-22 that by a laying of

Hands on the Scapegoat, the sins of the people will be transferred to that animal. **I'll tell you** - to think that people take this *stuff* literally boggles the mind. This theme of Blood Sacrifice along with the Casting Out of Demons, and such related nonsense (when accepted literally) is repeated throughout the bible – in the Old Testament and the New Testament.

The cosmic sun must pay homage to two hemispheres – the northern and the southern spheres. The suns safety, in a symbolical sense, can be guaranteed only through the *appeasement of both entities* – this goes to the philosophical core of dualism and expiation through sacrifice, which can be viewed as a payment, a ransom if you will. **The captured and bound Scapegoat** that is led into the wilderness as a Sacrifice to a jealous and merciless Demon is a mythological Copy of an astronomical Parallel – that is the descent of the sun into the depths of the southern hemisphere to it's death at Capricorn (the Winter Solstice). The slaughtered goat is the victim of a Vengeful Lord that will not allow his Subjects to escape without some taste of their blood. This is a mythological description of a material world – and the seminal foundation of religious Sacrificial and Atonement Concepts, from pre-Christian times to the present.

THE GOAT IS THE DEVIL

See this definition of the word Devil from dictionary.com

devil (Gr. diabolos), a slanderer, the arch-enemy of man's spiritual interest (Job 1:6; Rev. 2:10; Zech. 3:1). He is called also "the accuser of the brethen" (Rev. 12:10). In Lev. 17:7 the word "devil" is the translation of **the Hebrew _sair_, meaning a "goat" or "satyr"** *(Isa. 13:21; 34:14), alluding to the wood-daemons, the objects of idolatrous worship among the heathen. In Deut. 32:17 and Ps. 106:37 it is the translation of Hebrew _shed_, meaning lord, and idol, regarded by the Jews as a "demon," as the word is rendered in the Revised Version. In the narratives of the Gospels regarding the "casting out of devils" a different Greek word (daimon) is used. In the time of our Lord there were frequent cases of demoniacal possession (Matt. 12:25-30; Mark 5:1-20; Luke 4:35; 10:18, etc.).* Source: Easton's 1897 Bible Dictionary

Take note of the following artist conception of the devil (Pan, Satyr etc), drawn sometime in the 17th or 18th century I believe. The *True* symbolism of the devil (lower god) is conveyed in this picture. Note the goat legs and cloven hooves – the devil (goat) horns protruding from the creature's head. The blowing of the brass horn (trumpet) was a traditional part of the sacrificial ceremony.

Numbers 10:10
[10] *Also in the day of your gladness, and in your solemn days, and in the beginnings of your months,* **ye shall blow with the trumpets over your burnt offerings,** *and over the sacrifices of your peace*

offerings; that they may be to you for a memorial before your God: I am the LORD your God.

Figure 3: This creature is clearly fashioned after a Goat. Note the trumpet that was traditionally a part of the sacrificial ceremony

THE PASSOVER SACRIFICE

Both equinoxes are points of Sacrifice and penitence. The ceremonies of Passover and Easter are dominant as the sun crosses the *vernal* equinox. The basic symbolism is the same as at the autumnal equinox, however in the Passover and Easter themes the ideas of *Deliverance* and *Ransom* are more prominent. **This is understandable** in that the lower hemisphere represents captivity – so liberation and the payment of a Ransom fall right in line with an allegorical representation of the suns transit from the lower sphere into the higher sphere.

In a mythological context, a Ransom is paid to the Demon of the South for the release of the captive sun (Jesus, Israel). This symbolizes the release of the cosmic sun from the polarity of the South Pole or Winter Solstice over to the polarity of the North Pole[21] or Summer Solstice. **This is confirmed** in the following biblical passages.

Isaiah   43:3   through   Isaiah   43:4
³For I am the LORD thy God, the Holy One of Israel, thy Saviour: I

---

[21] In the Stellar phase of the symbolism the Poles are used for a reference instead of or in addition to the Solstices. We may review that point later in this or the next Volume of the Series.

gave Egypt for thy **ransom**, *Ethiopia and Seba for thee.* *⁴Since thou wast precious in my sight, thou hast been honourable, and I have loved thee: therefore will I give men for thee, and people for thy life.*

Hosea13:14
¹⁴I will **ransom** *them from the power of the grave; I will redeem them from death: O death, I will be thy plagues; O grave, I will be thy destruction: repentance shall be hid from mine eyes.*

Matthew   20:28
²⁸Even as the Son of man came not to be ministered unto, but to minister, and to give his life a **ransom** *for many.*

1   Timothy   2:6
⁶Who gave himself a **ransom** *for all, to be testified in due time.*

Isaiah 43:3-4 clearly states that **God** (upper cosmic region) **paid a ransom to Egypt** (lower cosmic region) - and the other verses are equally explicit. The payment of a ransom is a function carried out between contending forces – it is the price (sacrifice) that must be made to secure the release of the captive subject (sun, symbolized as Israel, Jesus).

I must reiterate, the biblical injunction requires that the **Passover** sacrifice be forever linked to the suns crossing of the equinoxes *which is indicated* as the 1ˢᵗ month of the religious year in the following verse.

Leviticus   23:5   through   Leviticus   23:8
⁵In the fourteenth day of the first month at even is the LORD'S passover. ⁶And on the fifteenth day of the same month is the feast of unleavened bread unto the LORD: seven days ye must eat unleavened bread. ⁷In the first day ye shall have an holy convocation: ye shall do no servile work therein. ⁸But ye shall offer an offering made by fire unto the LORD seven days: in the seventh day is an holy convocation: ye shall do no servile work therein.
Leviticus   23:12
¹²And ye shall offer that day when ye wave the sheaf an he lamb without blemish of the first year for a burnt offering unto the LORD.
Leviticus   23:14
¹⁴And ye shall eat neither bread, nor parched corn, nor green ears, until the selfsame day that ye have brought an offering unto your God: it shall be a statute for ever throughout your generations in all your dwellings.

Jesus is confirmed as a proxy for the Passover Lamb in the following verses,

1   Corinthians   5:7
⁷Purge out therefore the old leaven, that ye may be a new lump, as ye are unleavened. For even Christ our passover is sacrificed for us.

1 Timothy 2:5 through 1 Timothy 2:6
⁵For there is one God, and one mediator between God and men, the man Christ Jesus; ⁶Who gave himself a ransom for all, to be testified in due time.

I think that the linkage is clear – both Sacrificial Seasons are *inseparable* from the *equinoxes*; this is confirmed by the biblical passages that we have inserted. And the *Line of the Equinoxes*[22] is the border that divides the regions of the cosmos, as referenced from the planet earth. **Our seasons are measured** in accordance with the span of time that the sun spends above and below the *Line of the Equinoxes*. The Ancients represented these two divisions of Space allegorically (within the symbolism of their theology) as apposing Spiritual Powers. **The Higher God** *of Positive Polarity* symbolized the Northern Hemisphere. **The Lower God** *of Negative Polarity* symbolized the Southern Hemisphere. They saw the sun as a vassal of both hemispheres, caught in an endless cycle of

---

[22] That is, the Line (celestial equator) that intersects the equinoctial points

sacrificial atonement as it oscillated between the contending regions.

Chapter Four - Egyptian Origin of the Christ Myth

Unveiling Ancient Egypt as the original source of Astrological Mythology

The bible is a Registry of astronomical phenomena written in a mythological format. **All of the major religions** have been fashioned as reflections of astronomical phenomena. Hence the similarities in the histories of the various mythical demigods, such as Christ, Krishna, Buddha, Mithra, Quetzalcoatl and others are easily explained – they all symbolize the same cosmic interactions. The best and clearest evidence of this linkage *between religion and astrology* is found in the ancient history of Egypt. The Ancient Egyptians have bequeathed abundant information to us in testimony of their religious mythology – and the astrological connection is evident.

The astrological foundation of the *Virgin Birth of the savior demigod* is recorded in stone, on the walls of ancient Egyptian edifices and also papyruses. Not only are the astronomical correlations quite clear but also the biblical connections are striking. **Our task**, within this chapter, is to present reasonable evidence that supports our claim that Egyptian religion is fundamentally based on astronomy/astrology – and further to expose the *parallels of biblical symbolism* to both (Egyptian religion and astronomical phenomena). Of course, we all know that Egyptian religion was based on Sun worship, so by establishing linkage between the scriptures of ancient Egypt and the biblical scriptures – we will also automatically bring more credence to our allegations that Christianity and it's cohorts i.e. Judaism and Islam are religions that are based on Sun worship also.

There are four major divisions to scriptural symbolism and mythological symbolism in general, namely *Stellar, Lunar, Solar* and *Environmental.* Of course these four categories are often, if not inevitably, linked in the mythology. **We are primarily focused on solar symbolism**, that is the *description* of the *sun's movements* throughout the cosmos under the Type of mythological symbols. **Environment always has some effect** on the structure and focus of regional allegories. The methods incorporated by the Priesthoods (of diverse demographics and climates throughout the world) were to insert *their* people into the context of the mythology. **This, of course required that adjustments be made** to the tales so that the stories related to the culture and environment of the targeted audience.

Treasures Of The Nile

Egypt was and is unique among all cultures, in that their nation is over 90% desert, with no significant annual rainfall and only one major river to supply the essence of life – fresh water. Whether Egypt lived or died depended on the flow of the Nile River – and over time the Egyptians referred to the **Nile River** as their **Savior.** The Egyptians divided their year into three seasons of four months each that started with the *Inundation,* a general flooding of the Nile area, which happened to commence about the time of the summer solstice – followed by four months of rapidly receding water levels, leading to the final four months of near drought conditions.

The Egyptian calendar was a sidereal type, since the beginning of their Sothic year was pegged to the heliacal rising of the star Sirius. Of course, the calendar was based on a solar year of 365 ¼ days. This calendar was governed by the Sothic[23] Cycle. The beginning of the Egyptian calendar year and the Flooding of the Nile valley were concurrent with the summer solstice, more or less.

Usually the measurement of our year is based on the sun's crossing of a cardinal point – the cardinal points are the two

---

[23] See Appendix for more information

88

equinoxes and the two solstices. The Spring Equinox is the most prominent New Years date (historically speaking), but all four cardinal positions have been used to start the year at some time in history by various cultures. For example, Europeans have used both December 25 and March 25 as the first days of their calendar years. These dates (Dec. 25 and Mar. 25) are approximations of the winter solstice and the spring equinox. It is reasonable that a culture may choose a cardinal point for a New Years date that impacts most significantly on their environment.

Egypt does not experience a traditional winter season or rainy season – therefore the Spring Equinox (which usually signals relief from coldness and drought) did not impact the Egyptian environment as it might effect other cultures in different regions at different latitudes. The *Summer Solstice* signaled the *Rebirth* of the Nile (Inundation) – and this was symbolized as the Rebirth of the Egyptian mythical *Savior.* The Egyptians came face to face with the prospect of death by starvation and drought, in the Bottom half of their year, as the Nile receded to lower levels. The receding Nile occurred more or less concurrently with the fall of the sun below the equinoxes – so the sinking sun and the sinking Nile were in close relationship. The mythical devil of the Egyptians became the Desert itself, or some Heinous Demon that resided in the desert and consumed their sun and their Water (Nile) with each years passing, sort of like a Serpent that swallows it's prey whole. The Nile receded to it's lowest depths from Winter through Spring. The bouncing of the sun off of the *winter solstice* in late December was a sign of their god's *cosmic* rebirth (Horus/Osirus on Dec. 25) and conversely, the re-emergence of the **Nile (flooding)** from the depths of the equatorial swamps (that Sea of Reeds), near the time of the *Summer Solstice*, was a manifestation of their **god's rebirth** in the *Environmental* phase.

The Signs in the Heavens that signaled the Environmental re-birth of the Egyptian Savior (Nile River) was the **heliacal rising** of the Dog Star, **Sirius**. This is the way the ancient Egyptians saw it – the Star Sirius was the Mother of the Nile. The heliacal rising of that star signaled the coming flooding of the Nile (Egypt's Savior) – and when this sentiment was transposed into the Egyptian mythology, it became the virgin Mother Isis-Hathor giving birth to the Savior of (their) world. So we have a cosmic birth of the Egyptian Savior, at the Winter Solstice, **when the Sun** (that was cosmically (immaculately) impregnated at the Vernal Equinox) **gives birth to the newborn sun, mythical Horus** – this is the solar mythology, reflective of the transits of the sun. And we also have the birth of the renewed Savior, *the Flooding Nile* at the Summer Solstice – this is the Environmental Mythology, reflective of the seasonal and agricultural variations that accompany astronomical changes.

I have supplied the following graphic that will help us understand the heliacal rising of Sirius and the process leading up to the event. The Dog Star *Sirius* is located within the constellation of Canis Major. **Our focus is on the star Sirius** since this was the star that the ancient Egyptians looked to as an **Indicator** for the **Birth** of their **Savior** (Nile) at or about the time of the *Summer Solstice.*

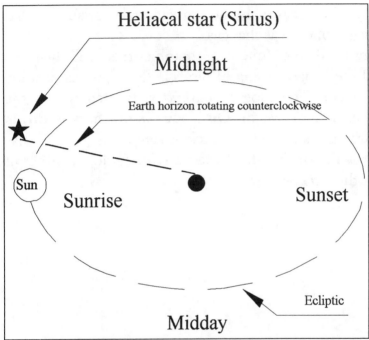

Figure 4: Ecliptic is *apparent* annual path of sun (counterclockwise) through zodiac around earth. Sun appears to cross all the constellations of the zodiac in the course of one year. Sirius is in Gemini sector, within the constellation called Canis Major. Sirius is Isis-Hathor in this phase of the mythos, mother of the Nile (Savior).

The apparent path of the sun annually through the zodiac is counterclockwise, as is indicated in the graphic. The eastward rotation of the earth is counterclockwise, as indicated in the graphic. The heliacal position of *Sirius* is to the West of the sun on the horizon — this means that the star is on the celestial border that divides Light from Darkness (as perceived from the earth), for the longitude on earth (at the horizon) that is turning toward (approaching) the first light of dawn. Hence, the appearance of the star *immediately preceding the dawn*, after which the dawning light of the sun will blot out it's (star) visibility is likened unto the star *rising with the sun* – such is the heliacal rising.

Of course, any star that was bright enough to be seen in the fading darkness of dawn could serve to indicate the sun's astronomical position – just below the horizon. But none could perform this service better than *Sirius* because it is the brightest star in the sky. The Egyptians needed to know *when* the sun approached the summer solstice because the sun, at it's highest declination of Plus 23 ½ degrees, signaled the flooding of the Nile Valley which the Egyptians likened to the annual **Re-birth of their God Savior (Nile).**

The Virgin Gives Birth

So we can readily see that the ancient Egyptians initiated a system (Sothic) that used a heliacal star (Sirius) to **announce** the *Birth of their Savior (Nile)* and the **Savior was born of a Virgin**. We must understand that the **Virgin Birth does not actually indicate the divinity** of the mother, although religiously centered people take it that way. The Priests who wrote these Tales were composing a *mythological Copy of an astronomical event or process.* I have already written in Book Two and elsewhere that Impregnation and/or Marriage is (oftentimes) *indicated* by Conjunctions of celestial entities and/or when celestial entities transit Cardinal Points. Under the aforementioned circumstances of conjunctions or transits – the Priests may select *mythological Male and Female symbols that will serve to represent the celestial entities,* in their conjunction phases and beyond. And of course the celestial event or process that follows the cosmic conjunction would (in the mythological symbolism) be represented as the *Offspring* of the selected mythical deities. **But,** in a case where the cosmic event (offspring) was *not preceded* by a noted celestial transit/conjunction, but rather seemingly generated by a *single celestial activity* – then such an event may have been produced by a Single parent (single noted celestial activity) and thus may be mythically represented as a Virgin birth - birth by one parent. **Also,** We find a lot of incest depicted in the bible and other mythologies – this is because mythical symbols that are *brothers and sisters* or *parents and children* in one chronology (time span) may cosmically transit each other in subsequent astronomical chronologies. The continued *re-transiting or re-occulting* of celestial entities creates a mythological representation of marriage and/or sex (between entities that may have become related because of prior celestial conjunctions) and consequently the mythological tales will unavoidably reflect this overlapping situation as marriage or sex between close relatives – but these (incestuous relationships) are mythological copies of repeated cosmic interactions (transits and conjunctions) between celestial entities.

EGYPTIAN RECORDS OF THE VIRGIN BIRTH

The following copies of Egyptian Relief's offer additional support to our premise – that the *Virgin Birth Concept* originated in Egypt. The following *Relief* reportedly dates from the 18th Dynasty, which spanned a period within the Astrological Age of Aries. The origination of the zodiac goes far back into prehistory. **The knowledge that the Ancients possessed of the Cosmos has not been improved upon**, to this date. By the time the Egyptian dynastic period commenced, around 3300 BC, the Heavens had been completed charted! Such charting cannot be done in a short time, considering the requirements of empirical investigations. Not to mention the need for advanced mathematical computations and explorations – they charted parts of the Heavens that are not visible from any part of Egypt. It (the astronomical mapping) was a Done Deal over 5,000 years ago! The storehouse of astronomical knowledge that the Ancients accumulated indicates many, many thousands of years of observation and calculations. **Our present day charts of the Heavens are based on the charts of the Ancients.** Modern astronomy is, to some extent, the re-discovering of what the Ancients have already calculated and recorded. The divisions of Time - seconds, minutes, days, weeks, months, years, etc. were all in use before modern civilization became modern.

The following Relief has four sections, which I have numbered. **Frame 1** pictures the Annunciation, **Frame 2** shows the bestowment and confirmation of the blessed conception, **Frame 3** pictures the delivery of the child god, **Frame 4** depicts the enthronement, adoration and giving of gifts to the savior. The participants in *Frame one* are Taht (moon deity) and the blessed virgin; *Frame two* – Kneph (Ram headed deity), the virgin and Hathor (fertility goddess), *Frame three* – the virgin sits atop a *birth stool* and the newborn savior is held by midwives and attendants, *Frame four* – the child god on throne with visitors in adoration.

This sequence of events is in direct parallel to the events that surrounded the birth of the mythical *Jesus Christ*. The association is explicit in the first and second chapters of Luke, which I referenced in an earlier portion of this book. It is clear that both myths (Egyptian and Christian) have the same astronomical base. The astronomical base is celestially located in the sector of *Gemini* – other constellations within this sector are *Argo Navis, Canis Major* and *Canis Minor*. **See Appendix of Book One** for a Listing of stars located within the sector of Gemini.

The constellation Canis Major means Large Dog and *Sirius* is the major star within this asterism. *Sirius*, as the blessed virgin mother, is already given to us in Egyptian history – so that connection with the constellation of *Canis Major* is established. The **Savior** that is born *under the Environmental mythology* is the **Nile** itself, the Savior of the land of Egypt. A great reference on stars is the Book: **Star Names, Their Lore and Meaning** *by Richard H. Allen,* the following information is given under the subject heading for *Canis Major – he sites Plutarch as a reference for Sirius being anciently regarded as the bringer of the Nile Flood, he Sites with references that Sirius was symbolized as Isis- Hathor at* **Thebes** *in Egypt as early as 3285 BC. He writes,* "*Sirius was worshipped, too, as Sihor, the Nile star,*" – **another quote** "*for the Egyptians always attributed to the Dog –star the beneficial influence of the inundation that began at the summer solstice;*" – **Also within the constellation of Canis Major**, we have the star *Mirzam* which means **Announcer.** This is vivid – the *Annunciation* and the *Virgin* are clearly associated with stellar entities. **The star** *Adhara* - it means **Virgin**, is also located within this constellation of the Dog.

It is clear that cosmic entities and events, within ancient Egypt, were symbolized as mythical deities - and the same holds true for our modern biblical symbolism. The bible is a Registry of Astronomical Phenomena written in a mythological format.

Figure 5: 1 - Annunciation 2 - Conception, Pregnancy 3 - Birth 4 - Adoration

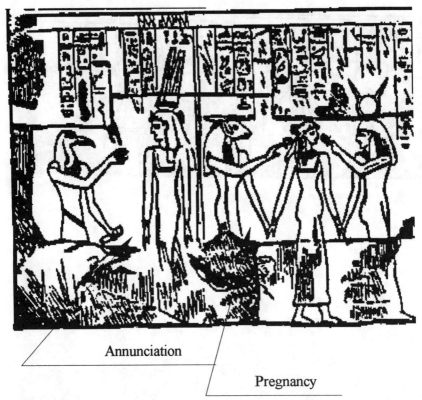

Annunciation

Pregnancy

Figure 6: **Enlargement** -Taht informs Queen that she is blessed Virgin - Next frame, Kneph and Hathor carry forth with blessing - Queen shows pregnancy

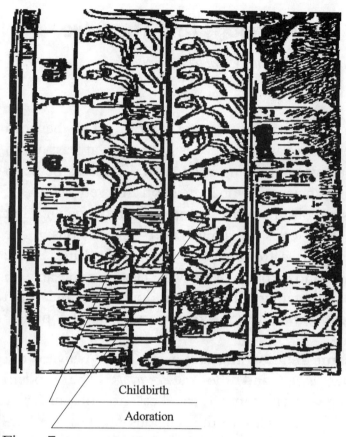

Childbirth

Adoration

Figure 7: **Enlargement** - Queen on top birthing stool and child is delivered - Next frame, child on Throne and hailed as newborn King and gifts are offered

Chapter Five - Astrology And The Bible

Expounding on various Correlations between Astronomy and Biblical Scripture

We found in the previous chapter that the link between astronomy and Egyptian religion was not veiled, at least not in today's perspective i.e. looking back on it. The links between astronomy and ancient Egyptian religion are very vivid. Of course the symbolism seems complex and intriguing but nevertheless the celestial connection is obvious. The representations of astronomical entities as deities were straightforward and explicit. This was clearly noticeable in their writings and graphics. There is no doubt as to the origin of the Egyptian earthly deities – they were mythical copies of celestial entities.

The exact same relationship still exists today between our *modern religious deities* and the *cosmic lights*. The modern (initiated) clergy has done their best to obscure this astronomical/biblical link and the religious fanatics (e.g. Fire and Brimstone preachers) just don't know any better. However, because the correlations within the bible are so plentiful, we are able to overcome the obscurities without much difficulty, if we are persistent.

Concept Of Heaven And Hell

At this time I would like to explore the Popular Concept of *Heaven, Hell* and the *Judgment* along with the accompanying belief in a future *Eternal Life* or *Eternal Damnation*. The origin of this myth is clearly exemplified in the stellar mythos.

There are more elements within the *stellar mythology* than the *solar* and **it is important** that the Reader possess, at least, a basic understanding of our celestial coordinate system in order to properly understand the symbolic interpretations. So I would like to suggest that the reader take note of the following *Terms* – and if these *Terms* are Unfamiliar, please review them in our Glossary before proceeding. **I highly recommend that these Terms be reviewed in a Handbook on astronomy**. I always have one at my side when studying these issues.

The following geographical/astronomical terms may be used in my effort to explain the **Stellar Link** to the **Judgment, Heaven and Hell concept**:

North Pole, South Pole, Ecliptic North Pole, Ecliptic South Pole, Earth Rotational Axis, Latitude, Longitude, Equator, North Celestial Pole, South Celestial Pole, Declination, Right Ascension, Celestial Equator, Ecliptic, Horizon, Altitude, Azimuth, Heliacal, 90 degree Arc, 180 Degree Arc, 360 Degree Arc, Nadir, Zenith, Equinox,

Solstice, Meridian, Prime Meridian, Sidereal Year, Tropical Year, Tilt of the Earth's axis to the Plane of it's orbit, Orbit,(Revolve) Revolution, Rotation, Celestial Canopy[24].

Mythology is a symbolic copy of astronomical phenomena; therefore it is vital that the reader first has understanding of the original (basic astronomy) before attempting to evaluate the copy (mythology). As I have said, there are four categories of mythological symbolism – *Stellar, Lunar, Solar* and Environmental. The evolution of mythological symbolism started with the stellar and evolved into lunar and finally solar. *Environmental Mythology* is a term that I have coined that I believe aids in the clarification of the three traditional categories – it can't stand alone, but rather blends in with the others. Perhaps other Researchers have used the term also – I don't know, as I have not read everything there is to read on this subject.

Stellar mythology is reflective of the movements or apparent movements of the stars. The Concepts of Heaven and Hell and Resurrection are clearly exemplified in the apparent movement of the stars as perceived from earth. **We will first explain the astronomical facts** and then, with the help of the bible as a reference – we will prove the mythological

---

[24] See the Glossary for this term

symbolism that was applied to the astronomical phenomena. This symbolism, when taken literally has caused many to believe in a Life after Death and a Heaven of eternal Bliss or Hell of eternal Damnation, which is pure fantasy. We will show that it is all in the stars – that the Ancients were symbolizing the death and resurrection of elements within the cosmos and astronomical coordinates that demark sections of Space that they likened to Regions of Hell or Heaven in their mythology.

We will explain the astronomical facts in two phases – first *East to West*, in terms of the westward movement of the stars due to the eastwardly rotation of the earth. We will focus on the following graphic that I have labeled **Canopy** to help us in our explanations. The second phase of our evaluations will be *North to South*, in terms of the northern and southern polar regions, and the situations of the stars located therein. We will use the graphic that I have labeled **Sky Dome** to aid in the explanations. After these two phases, our third phase will be an interpretation of the mythology as symbolically applied to the astronomical facts.

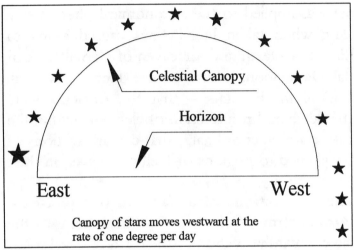

Figure 8: **Canopy** - Sidereal day is about 4 minutes less than the solar day. This causes a portion of the stars (1 degree of arc) to drop from visibility each 24 hours.

ASTRONOMICAL FACTS

View the Graphic labeled **Canopy** – The horizon is the position of an observer on Earth. As the earth rotates eastward, in the evening, at the rate of 15 degrees every hour – the east-west locations of the stars overhead change at the same rate (15 degrees per hour). This means that any star that is directly above you on the meridian, at say 12 midnight, will after 2 hours be 30 degrees to the west of the meridian. During the course of the evening, stars are constantly rising (coming into view) on the Eastern Horizon and Setting (disappearing from view) on the Western Horizon. In the Picturesque language of the Ancients – the Rising stars were Birthing stars and the Setting stars were Dying stars. This will be explained in detail later. The sky is a dome with stars painted upon it. The positions of these stars are fixed, and do not change in relation to each other[25]. Therefore we must think of the sky as moving canopy or curved ceiling, if you will, that revolves around the earth at a set rate. The sky has been mapped by grouping fixed stars into blocks of stars called constellations. The Ancients sorted the cosmos into 48 such constellations and named them. The 12 constellations that line the path of the sun's ecliptic are called the zodiac.

Also, due to the fact that the sidereal day is about four minutes less than the solar day, the celestial canopy of viewable stars (stars visible from one geographical coordinate[26] within one 24 hour period) shifts one degree westward within a days Time span of 24 hours – this shift will total 360 degrees in a years time (365 ¼ days) i.e. a complete *revolution* of the

---

[25] Actually there are relational changes after many thousands and millions of years. Also the precession causes coordinate changes but the positions of stars are calculated within periods and are considered Fixed for that span of time.

[26] Geographical coordinate is the point of intersection of the longitude and latitude of the observer

---

viewable night sky over any observer's coordinate. **In regards to daily time keeping**, a point on earth at a particular longitude will make a complete 360-degree *rotation* relative to a distant star as a marker in about 23 hours 56 minutes (sidereal day) – but yet have to *rotate* an additional one-degree (a time span of about 4 minutes) to reach re-alignment with the sun. This is because the earth is *revolving* around the sun at a little less than a degree a day, and consequently the Line of alignment with the sun (at the meridian), for any geographical coordinate on earth, is shifting accordingly, in step with the changing orbital position of the earth relative to the sun. In keeping with this scenario, the heliacal risings move eastward by one-degree a day and concurrently the Night Canopy of viewable stars shift westward by one-degree a day; so that after one year the cycle (of heliacal risings) completes itself i.e. returns to the hour / degree of Right Ascension from whence the year started. **Precession has an effect**, since degrees of Right Ascension are measured eastward from the Vernal Equinox, but this effect is disregarded[27] (in the mythical symbolism) until it appreciates to one degree or more, which takes 70-72 years.

---

[27] Of course the Ancients did not totally disregard anything but we need not focus on minutia at this point i.e. the variance of 1/72 of a degree a year

View the Graphic labeled **Sky Dome** – This graphic assumes the position of an observer on earth is at 30 degrees north latitude. The Line FC is the horizon of the observer, therefore the portion of the sky marked by the Arc FBC is the Limit of the Sky Dome visible (at night) to the observer at 30 degrees North latitude. The Line AD is the Rotational Axis of the earth extended into the cosmos – the rotation is from right to left – Arc AED is the side of earth facing the sun and Arc ABD is the Night Sky. Line G1G2 shows the position of the observers horizon during daylight hours. Arc G1AF and Arc G2DC are the North and South circumpolar regions respectively. The Southern circumpolar region is *outside of the visibility* of our observer and the Northern circumpolar region *remains constantly above the horizon* of our observer. Line EB is the earths equator extended into the cosmos, hence celestial equator.

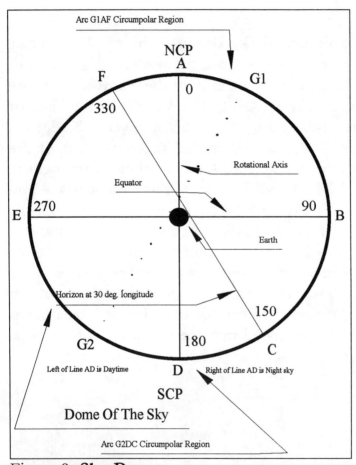

Figure 9: **Sky Dome** - Line FC is the Horizon for an Observer at Latitude 30 degrees, Line G1G2 is the position of the Horizon in Daytime, 0 (360), 90, 150, 180, 270, 330 are degree markers

MYTHOLOGICAL COPY OF NATURAL PHENOMENA

The theme of *Death and Resurrection* prevails throughout nature and is easily recognized. The Ancients saw it daily in the death of the sun each evening as it sank below the western horizon, leaving them in darkness. The sun is resurrected each morning on the opposite side of the world as it rises above the eastern horizon. This is nature's number one example of life (light) after death (darkness). Of course, the theme is obviously played out in the change of seasons – the winter brings death to the remnants of a verdant summer, but alas when the spring and summer return Life is miraculously renewed. The Ancients also saw this theme exemplified in the Heavens in the life and death cycles of the stars. Each night a Line of stars (covering 1 degree of *Right Ascension*) had their heliacal *setting* with the sun, that is the stars appeared briefly on the western horizon as the sun's light faded and night prevailed – but then disappeared below the western horizon, *and were not seen the next night* and not for many more nights, until they were resurrected. They, in a mythological sense, had died and entered into an Underworld of Purgatory, a valley of trials and Tests. When these cosmic lights finally reappeared (after some months below the horizon of the observer) on the eastern horizon in the evening sky, it was a validation that they had

Mythologically passed through the gate of judgment and were now among the resurrected.

This ancient concept is reflected in the Catholic belief in Purgatory –

See quote from Dictionary.com

purgatory n 1: a temporary condition of torment or suffering: "a purgatory of drug abuse" 2: (theology) a place where Roman Catholics think those who have died in a state of grace undergo limited torment to expiate their sins Source: *Easton's 1897 Bible Dictionary*

The ancient Egyptians were probably the first to institutionalize this Concept – that death was a passage to resurrection in a higher Life, but the reward came only after the Aspirants had overcome Trials and Tests and otherwise proven their sincerity and steadfastness.

The *Egyptian Book Of The Dead* contains a vivid description of the Trials and Tribulations of the deceased as they travel through the Underworld of Amenti, hoping to be granted a blessed entrance into the next life.

The Dead were alleged to have recited special hymns and prayers that were designed to ward off the evil intents of the demons and to help them gain a favorable judgment before the Lords of Purgatory, the Underworld. The Festival – *All Souls Day* was an ancient Roman Catholic holiday dedicated to prayer and almsgiving in an effort to help the Dead in their passage through Purgatory. This festival occurs a couple of days after Halloween. The parallels between these and the ancient Egyptian customs are clear.

The fact that these festivals are celebrated after the sun enters the underworld (the region below the equinoxes) evidences the reality of their true symbolism in the solar mythos; that is the trials and tribulations of the sun as it journeys through it's purgatory. This period of tribulation is actually experienced by the inhabitants of earth as we struggle to survive the severity of the winter season caused by the sun's descent into the valley of the celestial underworld.

This *Concept* of death as an *interval* between stages of material and spiritual Life as well as a form of purification by entrance into purgatory is a *mythological copy of an astronomical fact*. **The**

Ancients fashioned their religions this way – they formulated their mythical theology in direct correlation to astronomical phenomena. **The core of the mythological symbolism always remains the same**, regardless of the astronomical base that is being reflected. The *resurrection myth* copies nature in terms of the seasons - it copies the daily cycles of the sun, and it copies the stellar cosmos that we are now reviewing. Of course all of these are in parallel to the solar mythology that we have already reviewed – the trials of the solar sun beneath the equinoxes (which we covered in the prior chapters) is a cosmic parallel to the above. The **aspects** of the Southern Hemisphere *(region beneath the equinoxes)* as related to the Solar Symbolism and the **aspects** of the *region below the horizon* in the Stellar Symbolism are similar.

THE MYTHS OF HEAVEN AND HELL ARE ROOTED IN THE STELLAR MYTHOLOGY

Let us examine the characteristics of the mythological Hell – in so doing we will form a basis for comparison with the astronomical correlations I shall present. The Ancients viewed Hell as a Prison in their symbolism. The bible refers to hell as a Pit, Grave, a place of Captivity where souls are punished and held apart. The *Stellar Hell* is in parallel to the *Solar Hell.* The *Solar* Hell is the region *below the equinoxes* where Trials and

Tribulations take place, where transgressors are chastened and the same holds true for the Hell of the Stellar symbolism, howbeit the region of the Stellar Hell is more confined.

See Definition of Hell from Dictionary.com

hell derived from the Saxon helan, to cover; hence the covered or the invisible place. In Scripture there are three words so rendered: (1.) Sheol, occurring in the Old Testament sixty-five times. This word sheol is derived from a root-word meaning "to ask," "demand;" hence insatiableness (Prov. 30:15, 16). It is rendered "grave" thirty-one times (Gen. 37:35; 42:38; 44:29, 31; 1 Sam. 2:6, etc.). The Revisers have retained this rendering in the historical books with the original word in the margin, while in the poetical books they have reversed this rule. In thirty-one cases in the Authorized Version this word is rendered "hell," the place of disembodied spirits. The inhabitants of sheol are "the congregation of the dead" (Prov. 21:16). It is (a) the abode of the wicked (Num. 16:33; Job 24:19; Ps. 9:17; 31:17, etc.); (b) of the good (Ps. 16:10; 30:3; 49:15; 86:13, etc.). Sheol is described as deep (Job 11:8), dark (10:21, 22), with bars (17:16). The dead "go down" to it (Num. 16:30, 33; Ezek. 31:15, 16, 17). (2.) The Greek word hades of the New Testament has the same scope of signification as sheol of the Old Testament. It is a prison (1 Pet. 3:19), with gates and bars and locks (Matt. 16:18; Rev. 1:18), and it is downward (Matt. 11:23; Luke 10:15). The righteous and the wicked are separated. The blessed dead are in that part of hades called paradise (Luke 23:43). They are also said to be in Abraham's bosom (Luke 16:22). (3.) Gehenna, in most of its occurrences in the Greek New Testament, designates the place of the lost (Matt. 23:33). The fearful nature of their condition there is described in various figurative expressions (Matt. 8:12; 13:42; 22:13; 25:30; Luke 16:24, etc.). Source: Easton's 1897 Bible Dictionary

Also take note the following Definitions. **I have highlighted portions** of these definitions that go to the core of the Stellar symbolism i.e. an unseen region, a confined portion of Space.

Quote from Dictionary.com

sheol *(Heb., "the all-demanding world"* = *Gr. Hades,* **"the unknown region "**)*, **the invisible world** of departed souls.* <u>Source</u>: *Easton's 1897 Bible Dictionary*

hades that which is out of sight, a Greek word used to denote the state or place of the dead. All the dead alike go into this place. To be buried, to go down to the grave, to descend into hades, are equivalent expressions. In the LXX. this word is the usual rendering of the Hebrew sheol, the common receptacle of the departed (Gen. 42:38; Ps. 139:8; Hos. 13:14; Isa. 14:9). This term is of comparatively rare occurrence in the Greek New Testament. Our Lord speaks of Capernaum as being "brought down to hell" (hades), i.e., simply to the lowest debasement, (Matt. 11:23). It is contemplated as a kind of kingdom which could never overturn the foundation of Christ's kingdom (16:18), i.e., Christ's church can never die. In Luke 16:23 it is most distinctly associated with the doom and misery of the lost. In Acts 2:27-31 Peter quotes the LXX. version of Ps. 16:8-11, plainly for the purpose of proving our Lord's resurrection from the dead. David was left in the place of the dead, and his body saw corruption. Not so with Christ. According to ancient prophecy (Ps. 30:3) he was recalled to life.

It is clear from the definitions above that Hell is a place of Confinement, a place that is Unseen - It has bars (borders) - it is the abode of the dead. Within mythological symbolism the terms death, sleep, hidden and darkness are often synonymous or similar in their indications. All of these terms indicate that something is lifeless, either because it can't be seen (detected) or because it doesn't show life (light/movement).

We are focused on the Stellar Symbolism, that is to say *religious symbolism* as a reflection of the apparent movement of the stars. The stellar mythos parallels the solar mythos. In the solar mythos the apposing regions of space are demarcated by the celestial equator – and this is always true. As we study the stars, the effects of the Horizon are brought more into focus and the Horizon of the observer becomes a level of demarcation between the apposing spheres or a regulating/limiting force on the boundaries of the apposing spheres (North Celestial Pole verses South Celestial Pole). Within the solar symbolism, the mythology is primarily reflective of the transits of the sun but within the stellar symbolism, the mythology is primarily reflective of the apparent movement of the stars.

The Stellar Mythological Hell, Hades, Sheol is the South Polar Region. The stars within confines of the south polar region are the mythical souls of hell. These circumpolar stars are locked in apparent orbits about the South Celestial Pole and this is the Bottomless Pit (the cosmos has no bottom) referred to in biblical scriptures. The mythological description of hell as a place of captivity and entrapment is on the mark. The South Celestial Pole is, in fact, a cosmic bottomless Pit.

This symbolical hell is a mythological copy of an astronomical fact.

Take a look at the Graphic labeled *Sky dome* – note the Arc G2DC – this is the celestial circumpolar region of the south, extending into the infinite universe. The arc (G2DC) measures 60 degrees[28]. The stars within this region are *never* visible to our observer whose Horizon crosses the cosmos at a 30 degree angle to the earth rotational Axis (Line AD).

This region is in perpetual darkness to our observer (situated at 30 degrees north latitude). The line G1G2 represents the horizon of the observer during daylight hours. Take note that the **intersection** of the day and night horizons (right above the earth glyph at the center of the graph) – when these radii are extended to the end of circle (dome), the subtended arc (G2DC) is part of a cone shaped area of Space. Of course, I am describing a 3 dimensional event with a 2 dimensional graph, but I think that with a little imagination you can perceive the cone. This area of Space (when considered within the stellar symbolism) carries the same significance as the region below the equinoxes in the solar symbolism. When the sun (as a mythical symbol) falls below the line of the

---

[28] Of course the size of the region of Dark Space is linked to the celestial coordinates of the observer. If this is vague I strongly suggest that the reader consult a handbook on astronomy

equinoxes into the southern hemisphere, it has been Mythologically captured, chastened, entered into a condition of tribulations and trials. **When the stars fall below the horizon** into the zone of darkness, their fate is identical to the fate of the sun as a mythical symbol. The same symbolism that applies to the sun within the solar mythology is applicable to the stars within the stellar mythology, with practical adjustments.

And it follows that the *Stellar* region of the North Celestial Pole is **Mythologically identical** to the *Solar* Northern Hemisphere. The Pole Star is the mythological Throne of Heaven and the circumpolar stars are Angels and residents of heaven. **Let's view** the graphic labeled **Sky Dome** – The Arc G1AF is the circumpolar region of the North Celestial Pole. This region is the reverse of the South Celestial Pole. The stars in this region never fall below the Horizon. The Horizon line is Line FC - The Pole Star is NCP. You can see on the graph that the subtended Arc G1AF and the Pole Star (NCP) are always above the horizon.

During the course of the *night* and the *year*, the stars located in the regions indicated by the Arcs G1BC and G2EF pass over the horizon[29] of the observer – they *Rise* and they *Set*

---

[29] During the year the stars visible at night will rotate between these to regions represented by the Arcs G1BC and G2EF. The stars within Arc G1AF never set.

throughout the year. But since the stars of the North Celestial Pole region are always above the horizon of our observer, they never set and are always visible – **Hence their lives are Eternal** – *These Stars never Die* – They Live forever in the presence of God (NCP) on his throne. **This is the Mythological Copy of an Astronomical Fact** – the mythical heaven of eternal life is no less than a *symbolical copy of the condition and status of the circumpolar stars* that never set (Die) below the horizon.

The mythical heaven where the blessed are alleged to ascend to after death and live forever is an allegory, reflective of the northern circumpolar stars. The Pit of hell is the region of southern circumpolar stars. See the following biblical passage

Isaiah 14:13 through Isaiah 14:15

13: For thou hast said in thine heart, I will ascend into heaven, I will exalt my throne above the stars of God: I will sit also upon the mount of the congregation, **in the sides of the north:** *14: I will ascend above the heights of the clouds; I will be like the most High. 15: Yet thou shalt be brought down to hell, to the* **sides of the pit.**

Actually the constellations of the polar regions revolve very gradually over a period of 25,920 years. You may refer to the

Appendix of Book One for a listing of the circumpolar constellations.

Epilogue

Epilogue - The Dichotomy Of Religion

Religion exists at two Levels – the *Exoteric* and the *Esoteric*.
To put it bluntly, the exoteric level is meant for the profane. It
says somewhere in the bible that one should not cast pearls
before swine i.e. Pearls of Wisdom before the unappreciative
or unprepared. This dualistic system of conveying Truth
under a veil of falsehood has been used by all sacerdotal
classes in all ages and cultures. **This sends a message to me**
- that long ago the Wise may have reached a general
consensus that the *average intellect* is not inclined to deal with
the Hard Truth. I think that they were correct, if indeed that
consensus was somehow reached, perhaps tacitly.
**The exoteric literal level of religious philosophy is pure
idiocy.** To think that the fantastic Tales of demons and multi-
headed monsters and miraculous events of every stripe, such
as making the sun stand still, dividing the Red Sea, destroying
the world by flood and all the other related nonsense is
accepted without hesitation, on the basis of Faith, is
astonishing. Nevertheless, it is so.

The Esoteric Level of religion is a Science that is mathematical, coherent, logical and provable. But this science of Truth is *veiled by the masque of mythology*. Some are repulsed by this masque and unfortunately turn away and denounce all concepts that support the possible existence of a *Creator God Force*. The great majority accepts the myth at face value – believe it or not. But fortunately, there are some that choose the path of *Investigation*, of which you and I are a part.

Within this vast incomprehensible universe, this planet indeed this solar system is no more than one grain of sand on one beach amongst trillions of other grains amongst trillions of other beaches. **This is astronomical fact, not hyperbole** – ask any astronomer whether the forgoing statement is true or not and they might say that I have *overstated our significance* within the universe. **Nevertheless, we have the gall** to take our Tribal gods that over time have been elevated to National gods and Regional gods (because of the political, financial, and military advances of their adherents) and appoint these fabled deities as the creators and sustainers of all that exist. How ridiculous this is!

Within the bible the biblical Editors give the name of god as **"I Am"**, which is the short form. The fuller expression was **"I Am Becoming" (Evolving).** I suggest that this is the best of names that any deity or person could possess. In keeping with the above, I consider myself a Religious Evolutionist – I, like you, am Searching, Investigating, Calculating, and Evaluating all relevant Information, in search of Truth. And I ask you – is there any religion greater than Truth?

Bibliography

The World's Saviors	Charles Vail
Age Of Reason	Thomas Paine
The World's 16 Crucified Saviors	Kersey Graves
The Golden bough	Sir James George Frazer
Ruin's Of Empires	C. F. Volney
Star Names, Their Lore And Meaning	Richard H. Allen
Christianity Before Christ	John G. Jackson
Pagan Origins Of The Christ Myth	John G. Jackson
Origin And Evolution Of religion	Albert Churchward
History Of The First Council Of Nice	Dean Dudley
Ancient Egypt, Light Of The world	Gerald Massey
Who Is This King Of Glory	Alvin B. Kuhn
The Worship Of Augustus Caesar	Alexander Del Mar

Cycles, Correlations, Notations

Definitions and Detailed Information on Cycles, Formulas and Terms

Appendix

Cycles
Years
Anomalistic year   (365 days 6 hrs 13 min 53.1 sec)

Eclipse year   346.642199

Sidereal Year   365.2564 (365 days 6 hrs 9 min 9.54 sec)

Synodic year   354.36

Tropical year   365.242199 (365 days 5 hrs 48 min 45.51 sec)

Months

Draconian month	27.21222 days
Sidereal month	27.32166 days
Synodic month	29.53059 days
Tropical month	27.32156 days

Day

Sidereal day	23 hours 56 minutes 4.09 seconds
Solar (mean) day	24 hours

Planetary Orbital Hierarchy

Saturn	29 years
Jupiter	12 years
Mars	687 days
Sun	365 days
Venus	224 days
Mercury	88 days
Moon	29 or 30 days

Calendars And Calendar Notes

Gregorian Calendar

A solar calendar introduced in 1582. Year contains 365.2425 days with a Leap year every 4th year. A century year is not a Leap year, unless it is evenly divisible by 400.

Jewish Calendar

The minute contains 18 Halakim (the Halakim is 3 1/3 seconds), the hour contains 1080 Halakim, the day contains 25,920 Halakim. The Jewish calendar is based on cycles of the moon, and the month normally alternates between 29 and 30 days. A Jewish Synodic month *averages* 29 days 12 hours 793 Halakim (29 days 12 hours 44 minutes 3 1/3 seconds or 29.530589 days). The Time-Span of the lunar Synodic month is a calculated number – it is the mean or average time of the moon's revolution about the earth. The actual time of revolution varies because of various astronomical influences. Consequently, the calculated New Moon and the visual New Moon are not always in harmony. Symbolism that refers to the calculated New Moon and/or the visual moon are both applicable under varying circumstances. The Dark Phase of the moon spans 2 days 5 hours 204 Halakim (2 days 5 hours 11 minutes 20 seconds). The Light Phase of the moon spans 27 days 7 hours 589 Halakim (27 days 7 hours 32 minutes

43.33 seconds). The regular Jewish (lunar) year[30] is 354 days 8 hours 876 Halakim (354.36 days or 354 days 8 hours 48 minutes 40 seconds). The regular Leap year is 383 days 21 hours 589 Halakim. The 19 year calendar cycle contains 6939 days 16 hours 595 Halakim.

The Metonic cycle of 19 years is used to reconcile the Jewish Synodic month to the Tropical year (365.242199 days or 365 days 5 hours 48 minutes 45.51 seconds). The Metonic cycle contains 235 Synodic months (235 times 29.530589 days = 6939.688415 days). Nineteen Tropical years contain 6939.601781 days (19 times 365.242199 days = 6939.601781 days). The discrepancy between the two cycles (lunar and tropical) is only about 2 hours over a period of 19 years[31].

It is necessary to include Intercalated days and months into the lunar calendar so as to harmonize it with the tropical years within the Metonic cycle. The adjustment procedures are rather meticulous and need not be discussed within this book. The Metonic cycle contains 19 years (12 Common years and 7 Leap years). The Common year contains 12 lunar months for

---

[30] The Hebrew year when calibrated to the Tropical year equated to a solar year of 365.2468 days.

[31] When the Metonic Cycle is calculated by 365.2468 days to the year, the 2 cycles match exactly to 2 decimals at 6939.68 days

a total of 353-355 days. The Leap year contains 13 lunar months for a total of 383-385 days. Leap years occur in the 3rd, 6th, 8th, 11th, 14th, 17th, and 19th year of the Metonic cycle. The Jewish New Year (Rosh Hashanah) begins with the month of Tishri, in the Fall of the year, close to the Autumnal Equinox. Passover (Pesach) begins about the 14th of Nisan near the Vernal Equinox. The beginning of the Jewish year is pegged to the autumnal equinox, however you may, at times detect symbolism that reflects the years' commencement at the vernal equinox - both may be accurate depending on the focus and application of the allegory. The Ecclesiastical Year is pegged to a series of festivals that commence with the Passover observance that occurs near the vernal equinox.

WEEKS

The Names of our weekdays are correlated to the nearest planets and sun.

Planet Correlations

Sunday	Monday	Tuesday	Wednesday	Thursday	Friday	Saturday
Sun	Moon	Mars	Mercury	Jupiter	Venus	Saturn

Weekdays Sequence

This can be traced to the ancient Egyptian system of assigning a planet as ruler of each hour of the day, *and the day being named after the planet that rules the First Hour[32] of the day.* The Hierarchy of the planets is determined by their orbital time:

Saturn	Jupiter	Mars	Sun	Venus	Mercury	Moon
29 years	12 years	687 days	365 days	224 days	88 days	29 days

By calibrating the cycle of 7 days to the cycle of 24 hours, we find that by starting with Saturn as number one and counting through all the planets (1-7, in accordance with their hierarchy) within the limit (1 to 24 hours), that in turn the sequences of the Number one "1" return the planets in our current weekday order. For example if we count Saturn as the first hour of the day, it will renew at 8, 15, and 22, with Jupiter as 23 and Mars as 24(within the limit of 1 to 24) and consequently the next number one "1" will fall to the Sun (Sunday) as and ruler of the first hour of the next day and therefore the designated name for the next day. By continuing this process we will return in their order the Moon (Monday), Mars (Tuesday) and so on.

---

[32] With this system, the start of the day may be 12:AM

The Jewish week has 7 days, the first day of the week is Sunday and the Sabbath is Saturday; The Day/Date starts at 6 PM. The Seven Day Week is, as far as I can tell, an artificial cycle i.e. it does not reflect a natural astronomical cycle. Nevertheless, the 7 is a crucial component of the Jewish Calendrical system. The mathematical formula by which the calendar is calibrated requires the use of the number 7 – the number 7 is not arbitrary.

MONTHS

The Jewish months are *Tishri, Heshvan, Kislev, Tevet, Shevat. Adar, Nisan, Iyar, Sivan, Tammuz, Av, Elul.* Months are categorized as Deficient (29 days) or Complete (30 days). Tishri, Shevat, Nisan, Sivan, and Av are 30 (full) day months. Tevet, Adar, Iyar, Tammuz and Elul are 29 (deficient) day months.

The months of **Heshvan and Kislev** vary between 29 or 30 days. The length of a common year may vary between 353-355 days and a Leap Year between 383-385 days, so the months of **Heshvan** and/or **Kislev** are used to make the required adjustments. In a Abundant year a day is added to the month of **Heshvan** and In a Deficient year a day is subtracted from the month of **Kislev**. Regular years are 354 or 384 days, Deficient years are 353 or 383 days, Abundant years are 355 or 385 days.

JEWISH FESTIVALS

Rosh Hashanah, New year festival commemorating the creation of the world (actually the start of the Hebrew calendar cycle), takes place in the Fall near the autumnal equinox – Tishri 1.

Yom Kippur, Day of Atonement – Tishri 10. On this day the believers seek forgiveness in prayer and fasting for their sins. Actually this festival represents a Blood sacrifice to the Satan Deity of the Underworld - See Chapter Three.

Passover, Commemorates Israelites liberation from slavery in Egypt and crossing of the Red Sea . Actually symbolizes the ascension of the Sun above the vernal equinox

Julian Calendar

A solar calendar introduced in 45 BC. Year contains 365.25 days with an intercalary day every fourth year.

Julian Period

Chronological system used to circumvent the possible confusion in trying to determine the accurate date of a historical event. The cycle is 7980 years and the first year was placed at January one 4713 BC. The years are consecutively numbered from that date without reference to weeks or months.

Cycles, Multiyear

Callipic Cycle

A period of 4 Metonic cycles, consisting of 441 Hollow months (29 days) and 499 Full (30 days) months. It totals 27,759 days or 76 years at 365.25 days a year.

Cycle Of The Nodes

This is a period of 18.61 years (about 230 Lunations). In this period of time, the Line Of the Nodes makes one complete revolution. A nodical year is 346.642199 days (the time it takes for the sun to complete one apparent revolution of the shifting Nodes). This period is 18.6 days less than the Tropical year (365.242199 days).

The Nodical month or Draconian month measures the time it takes the moon to make one complete revolution through the nodes (i.e. when the moon intersects the sun's ecliptic). A nodical month is 27.21222 days.

Demigod Cycle

This is a cycle of 33 years. This is the Time that it takes to reconcile the difference between the solar tropical year (365.242199 days) and the lunar Synodic year (354.36709 days). There are 11(10.875119) days difference between the two cycles. Therefore, to determine the number of years it takes the two cycles to repeat at the same point "1", we divide the larger cycle (365 days) by the Difference (11 days) between the two cycles and that gives us a result of about 33.

This means that since the lunar Synodic cycle is losing 11 days per year on the tropical year, that in 33 years the two cycles will be reconciled back to a point of intersection whereas the first days of both cycles are more or less in correspondence.

This meeting of the cycles (Calendars) at the point where both commence represents the death of the old cycle and the simultaneous renewal (rebirth) of a new demigod cycle. So Jesus (the sun god) living 33 years actually represents the number of years necessary for the lunar calendar to cycle through the solar calendar. The Islamic calendar is a perfect example of the span of the Demigod cycle.

DEMIGOD REIGNING OR TEACHING FOR 3 YEARS

This represents the number of years it takes to reconcile the lunar Synodic year to the tropical year by a method of intercalation. The lunar cycle loss of 11 days a year to the tropical cycle accumulates to about one tropical month in 3 years time. Therefore the two cycles can be more or less synchronized by adding a 13th month to every 3rd lunar year.

So placing a limit of three years or so on the reign of the demigod is actually an instruction to add a Leap month to the lunar calendar after 3 years, so as to prevent an unacceptable dislocation of the seasons. The Jews have maintained this system to this day.

Intercalations and Adjustments

The Ancients developed a system of inserting Units of time (i.e. day(s), week, month, year) into a calendar in order to keep it correctly calibrated to a larger cycle.

There are 3 or 4 primary modes of timekeeping that must be reconciled on an ongoing basis so as to keep our calendars and charts as close to accuracy as possible, at any given point in time. This requires the periodic adjustment of Minor cycles to Major cycles.

The *Following* is a Model that does not cover all the possible adjustments. However, biblical symbolism touches on these correlations and it is possible to manipulate these proportions (or ratios) and others not herein noted, to decipher many biblical allegories.

TROPICAL YEAR TO SIDEREAL YEAR, WITH FOCUS ON THE GREAT YEAR

There is a difference of 20 minutes 24 seconds in the span of the Tropical year and the Sidereal year. Of course the Sidereal year is the longer span. In order to keep track of the rate of precession as defined by celestial markers (stars), Star Maps and Allegory must be updated so as to reflect the changes in the position of the equinoxes. *The 20.4 minutes of time represents about 1/72 degree of arc (.013888 degrees).* **As time progresses,** the symbolism must be adjusted to fit the New celestial positioning. An adjustment of 30 days in the position of a star *in relation to the equinox* is equivalent to 30 degrees of arc and so an adjustment of one day in the position of a star in relation to the equinox is equivalent to one degree and so forth. Seconds are disregarded at this stage of the adjustment cycle. The 24 seconds would probably fit into another cycle of 3600 years. There are 86,400 seconds in a day, so 3600 times 24 = 86,400 would produce a whole day (degree) that could be adjusted after 3600 years.

The Following Table exemplifies some of the possibilities you may encounter in biblical symbolism. We should remember that in this phase of the Stellar symbolism – even though we are dealing with *Units of Time* that *Degree Units(arc) are also indicated,* as explained above.

CYCLE	MULTIPLE	ADJUSTMENT
72 years	72 times 20 = 1440 min.	One day
504 years	504 times 20 = 10,080 min.	One (7 day) week
720 years	720 times 20 = 14,400 min.	One (10 day) week
1440 years	1440 times 20 = 28,800 min.	One (20 day) week/month
2160 years	2160 times 20 = 43,200 min	One (30 day) month

TROPICAL YEAR TO SIDEREAL YEAR, WITH REGARD TO KEEPING THE SEASONS IN SYNC

The Tropical year would drift out of season, if not adjusted periodically, because of the fractional day. The Tropical year is 365.242199 days.

CYCLE	INTERCALATION
4 years	Add one day
28 years	Add one (7 day) week
40 years	Add one (10 day) week
120 years	Add one (30 day) month

SYNODIC YEAR TO TROPICAL YEAR, WITH REGARD TO SEASONS

The lunar month is not naturally in sync with the solar year, therefore the lunar month must be mathematically manipulated into calibration with the solar cycle.

This is an Overview of the system adopted by the Ancients,

The lunar year of 354.36 days is about 11 days shorter than the solar year of 365.242199 days. Therefore, by inserting a month into the calendar at 3 year intervals, the lunar and solar cycles will be brought into close correspondence.

Furthermore, the Ancients determined that the Synodic cycle of 235 Lunations that totals 6939.688 days came into close correspondence with the solar cycle of 19 years (6939.6018 days). The discrepancy is only about 2 hours.

See Metonic Cycle, Also See Jewish Calendar for more information

Jupiter/Saturn Conjunction Cycle

This cycle renews itself every 2400 years. This is a 60-year cycle of 3 parts. The planets actually conjunct every 20 years and the third conjunction of the series is at a point 9 deg further east in the Zodiac than the conjunction that took place 60 years prior to the latest one.

Metonic Cycle

This is a period of 19 tropical years or 235 Lunations, which is used to reconcile lunar time to solar time. The cycles consist of 6939.688 days, 12 common years and 7 Leap years. Six of the Leap years contain an extra month of 30 days, and the 7th Leap year contains an extra month of 29 days.

The Metonic cycle is the chief method by which the lunar calendar is correlated to the tropical calendar. It could be said that the tropical year is the hour hand of the annual clock and the lunar month is an (out of sync) minute hand of the annual clock. The Ancients concluded universally that the best method by which to track the daily units of time were the phases of the moon. However it is equally important that we keep an accurate track of the tropical year, that controls and regulates the seasons and overall environment within which we may prosper or perish.

However, the lunar month and the tropical year do not coexist in natural harmony. It is impossible for any whole number of natural lunar months to equal a natural tropical year. But the Metonic cycle brings the two cycles of time measurement into correlation over a period of 19 years. Nineteen tropical years amount to 6939.60178 days and 235 Lunations equal 6939.688 days, bringing the two cycles within a fraction of absolute harmony.

Perihelion Shift Cycle

The Orbit of the earth around the sun is elliptical. The Perihelion indicates the **Point** in the path of the orbit, which is closest to the sun. The Perihelion shifts clockwise at a rate of about 1 deg in 60 years, actually making a complete revolution in approximately 21,000 years. Our closest approach to the sun presently occurs during the winter season.

Precession Cycle

The Egyptian Great Year – 25,920 years, divided into 12 zodiac sections of 2160 years each. The precession is measured by the westward movement of the vernal equinox. The rate is 50 seconds of arc per year, which accumulates to one degree in 72 years.

Saros Cycle

This Eclipse cycle is 6585.321124 days or about 18 years 11 1/3 days (18.0300117 years). It consists of 223 Lunations including 70 eclipses (41 solar, 29 lunar). At the end of this period, the cycle of eclipses repeats itself.

As I see it, this cycle does not focus on a correlation between the tropical and lunar cycles, but rather reconciles (at least) two of the Time Cycles by which lunar time is measured, namely the Synodic cycle (29.530589 days) and the Nodical cycle (27.21222 days). The Synodic cycle is the longest of the monthly lunar cycles – an easy explanation is that it measures from one full moon to the next full moon, or New moon to New moon. The Nodical cycle measures the time it takes the moon to make one complete revolution through the nodes (i.e. when the moon intersects the sun's ecliptic). We are able to measure the moon's revolution about the earth by various lunar cycle markers that include, among others, the stars, longitude, or perigee. However our focus, in this instance, is on the Synodic month and the Nodical month, as these relate to biblical symbolism.

The Saros cycle at 6585.321124 days, *when divided* by the length of a nodical month (27.21222 days) equals 242 whole months (decimalized is 241.9986728 months). *When we divide the Saros cycle* by the length of a Synodic month (29.530589 days) our result is, of course, 223 whole Synodic months (decimalized is 222.9999924). The difference between the two *monthly cycles of time* is 19 (242 minus 223 = 19).

One result of the harmony between these two monthly cycles *is that*, our astronomers are able to calculate the reappearance of the eclipses in exact precision. Once the position of the sun (at new moon) has revolved a complete circuit of the nodes over the 18 plus years, *the same sequence of eclipses that started the cycle is repeated, in kind.* Because of the partial 1/3 solar day (the length of the cycle in solar time is 18 years 11 1/3 days), the location of the *recommencement* of the Saros cycle, will have moved 120 degrees or so west of its previous start. Therefore it follows also, *that after three repetitions of the Saros cycle i.e. 669 Synodic months*, the point of longitude will have shifted westward 360 degrees back to its starting point 3 cycles ago i.e. about 54.09 years prior.

It is interesting to note that a series of 3 Saros cycles is about 54 years, and if we multiply 54 times 40 the result is 2160 years (an astrological age). Also 120 times 18 is 2160. Both

"40" and "120" are Significant Numbers in biblical symbolism.

Sothic Cycle

A sidereal cycle of 1460 years used by the ancient Egyptians and pegged to the heliacal rising of the star Sirius, of the constellation Canis Major. This cycle seems to measure the shift of the *commencement* of the Tropical year through 360 degrees. **In that,** without any adjustment being made to a 365 day calendar, it would take 1460 years for the First day of the year to travel completely through the calendar. Reportedly, at the end of this 1460 years, the Egyptians added a whole year to their calendar.

It is interesting to note that the Gregorian calendar parallels the Sothic system. The Gregorian calendar designates every fourth year as a Leap year, in which one day is added to the calendar (under most circumstances). Four years is actually 1460 days (4 times 365) – so the numbers match the Sothic system, but the units of time are different – days instead of years.

The Egyptian year consisted of 360 + 5 days. They observed 365 days but only counted 360 days in their calendar and the other 5 days were uncounted days dedicated to various deities. The year was separated into three seasons of 4 months each. The seasons were described according to their affect upon the environment - Inundation (overflowing of the Nile), Sowing (going forth) and Reaping (Deficiency, referring to a low Nile). Within the Sothic system, the year commenced near the time of the summer Solstice, mid July.

It is interesting to note that the aggregate of the uncounted 5 days over the period of 1460 years is 20 years. And if we subtract this 20 years from the 1460, the result is 1440 years which is $1/18^{th}$ of a Great Year. As far as I can tell at this point, the number 1440 is more useful in deciphering biblical symbolism than the number 1460.

I am of the opinion that the True focus of the Sothic system was the tracking of the Great Year of 25920 years. The Egyptians divided the Heavens into 36 Divisions (Decans) East to West marked by (heliacal) stars, of which *Sirius* was the number one Marker. I have read in more than one source that 3300 BC marked the exact correlation of the Summer Solstice and the Heliacal Rising of Sirius – such events usually herald the commencement of a Cycle. The fact that the Egyptian Dynastic System is alleged to have commenced circa 3285 BC would tend to support the assumption that the political leadership may have tied their ascension to power with the commencement of a New Age (cycle). Add to this that the Sothic calendar was only one among others used by the Egyptians then we may reasonably surmise that perhaps *Multiple Purposes* may have been involved, that is assuming that the other calendars were not based on regional/cultural considerations.

Correlations Of Seconds, Minutes and Halakim to Great Year

Biblical Symbolism is contained within the **Major Cycle of the Great Year i.e. 25,920 years.** All other cycles are *divisions* of this Major cycle. For example, an Astrological Age is 2160 years, hence 12 Astrological ages equal 25,920 years, which is One Great Year. Also an important cycle is 1440 years and 18 such cycles add up to 25,920 years. There are many other Lesser Cycles e.g. 72, 120, 360, and others. **It must be remembered** that some cycles are geared to harmonizing Lunar Time with Solar Time and may not fit these specifications. The Great year is pegged to the Precession of the equinoxes which completes it's revolution in 25,920 years. It is clear that the Ancients were Determined Not to loose track of their place in this Major Cycle. This obsession may carry implications of dread and apprehension concerning certain predictable sequences of severely adverse environmental trauma experienced by the inhabitants of earth.

So the Ancients devised units for daily and monthly timekeeping that are proportionate to the *Great Year* and *divisions of the Great Year.* And at times these common units of time are used metaphorically within the symbolism. **However,** it may be necessary to use a *Divisor* of 100 or perhaps 10 to reduce the Amount (of the Common Time Measurement) to the True number of years of a specified cycle.

The Symbolism does *not* use *measures of time* that are astronomically precise, but rather the numbers are *rounded off* for the sake of convenient computation. The System of the Ancients was to use rounded numbers in their computations and at intervals make adjustments. These intervals might span 72, 120, 360, 1440, 2160 or whatever years. **The ancient Festivals** were designated to *signal*[33] Calendrical adjustments. The *Root* number by which to Check the mathematical correlations to **Solar** Symbolism is the number "9". The resultant Figures (math numbers) obtained from the computation of numbers *focused* on deciphering **Solar** symbolism should be Evenly Divisible by nine. For instance, a cycle of 72 years could be a legitimate sub-cycle of the Great Year (25,920) because it is evenly divisible by nine – (72 divided by 9 = 8).

Seconds To Years

Great Year total is 25,920 years. One 30 Day Month (in seconds) correlates to One Great Year Cycle. Divisor for seconds is 100. Great Year has 12 Zodiac Divisions with each term (2160 years) representing an astrological Age.

DAY UNITS	SECONDS	YEARS
2 1/2 days	216,000 Seconds	2160 years
5 days	432,000 Seconds	4320 years
7 1/2 days	648,000 Seconds	6480 years
10 days	864,000 Seconds	8640 years
12 1/2 days	1,080,000 Seconds	10800 years
15 days	1,296,000 Seconds	12960 years
17 1/2 days	1,512,000 Seconds	15120 years

[33] A signal to the Sacerdotal Class who have been the true "Timekeepers" throughout history

20 days	1,728,000 Seconds	17280 years
22 1/2 days	1,944,000 Seconds	19440 years
25 days	2,160,000 Seconds	21600 years
27 1/2 days	2,376,000 Seconds	23760 years
30 days	2,592,000 Seconds	25920 years

Minutes To Years

Great Year is 25,920 years with 18 divisions of 1440 years each. Correlations of Minutes to Years does not require a Divisor. Correlation is Total at 18 days.

DAY UNITS	MINUTES	YEARS
One day	1440 Minutes	1440 years
Two Days	2880 Minutes	2880 years
Three days	4320 Minutes	4320 years
Four days	5760 Minutes	5760 years
Five days	7200 Minutes	7200 years
Six days	8640 Minutes	8640 years
Seven Days	10080 Minutes	10080 years
Eight Days	11520 Minutes	11520 years
Nine days	12960 Minutes	12960 years
Ten days	14400 Minutes	14400 years
Eleven days	15840 Minutes	15840 years
Twelve days	17280 Minutes	17280 years
Thirteen days	18720 Minutes	18720 years
Fourteen days	20160 Minutes	20160 years
Fifteen days	21600 Minutes	21600 years

Sixteen days	23040 Minutes	23040 years
Seventeen days	24480 Minutes	24480 years
Eighteen days	25920 Minutes	25920 years

Halakim To Years

Great Year is 25,920 years with 24 Divisions of 1080 years per cycle. Correlation is total at One day.

UNITS	HALAKIM	**YEARS**
One Minute	18 Halakim	18 years
One Hour	1080 Halakim	1080 years
Six Hours	6480 Halakim	6480 years
Twenty Four Hours	25,920 Halakim	25920 years

Hours To Years

The Symbolism counts Tropical years as 360 days, not 365 days. The 5 days were observed but not counted in part of the Egyptian history; these 5 days were observed as uncounted holidays dedicated to certain deities. I covered this matter in Book Two, Chapter Nine.

The Correlation is total at 25,920 years.

UNITS	HOURS	SYMBOLISM
90 Days	2160 Hours	Astrological Age
360 Days (1 year)	8640 Hours	Four Astrological Ages
1080 Days (3 years)	25920 Hours	One Great Year

Definitions And Author's Comments On Terms And Descriptions Used In This Book.

Glossary

Most Word definitions have been narrowed so as to focus on their usage within this book.

Altitude
The height of a celestial object in the sky when measured from the Horizon in degrees of arc

Aphelion
Point in the Earth's orbit that is farthest from the sun

Apogee
Point in the moon's orbit that is farthest from the earth

Arc
The curved outer line of a circle or ellipse that is, for our purposes, measured in degrees - 90 degrees is ¼ of the total circle, 180 degrees is ½ and 360 degrees is the complete circle. The Arc from the Zenith of the sky to the Horizon is 90 degrees. The Arc from the south horizon to the north horizon is 180 degrees, likewise from east to west. The complete circumference of the earth is 360 degrees.

Astrological Age

This is a cycle of 2160 years. Each cycle is named after a Zodiac sign and is pegged to the westward precession of the vernal equinox. Each Age covers 30 degrees of the arc of precession. Commencement Guidelines for each Age are as follows:

Pisces	-126 BC	Virgo	-13086 BC
Aries	-2286 BC	Libra	-15246 BC
Taurus	-4446 BC	Scorpio	-17406 BC
Gemini	-6606 BC	Sagittarius	-19566 BC
Cancer	-8766 BC	Capricorn	-21726 BC
Leo	-10926 BC	Aquarius	-23886 BC

Astronomical Unit

92,955,806 miles, which is the Mean distance between the earth and the sun - approximately 93,000,000 miles.

Axis (Earth Rotational Axis)

Straight Line between the North and South Poles around which the earth rotates

Azimuth

A measurement in degrees made horizontal to the Horizon from the North Pole clockwise to a maximum of 360 degrees – for example *Due East* has an azimuth of 90 degrees

Celestial Canopy

The sky above the horizons – this canopy is not constant but travels from East to West at the rate of 15 degrees per hour. Also, the group (canopy) of stars that are visible at night from any one location shift eastward by about one degree every 24 hours – making a complete revolution during the course of one sidereal year.

Celestial Equator

The extension of the earth's equator into the heavens

Day

Mean Solar Day	24 hours
Sidereal Day	23 hours 56 minutes 4 seconds

Declination

This is the angular distance measured north and south from the celestial equator. Lines of Declination are at right angles to Lines of Right Ascension

Dionysian Cycle

See Paschal Cycle

Ecliptic

This is the apparent path of the sun around the earth in the course of a year. The earth is actually tilted to the plane of it's orbit at 23.4523 degrees. This causes the declination of the sun to oscillate between minus 23.45 degrees at the winter solstice and plus 23.45 degrees at the summer solstice.

Moons orbit is tilted to the Ecliptic at 5 degrees 8 minutes

Ecliptic North Pole
Imaginary Pole perpendicular to the ecliptic and 23 ½ degrees from North Celestial Pole

Ecliptic South Pole
Imaginary Pole perpendicular to the ecliptic and 23 ½ degrees from South Celestial Pole

Epact
This is the age of the moon at the beginning of the solar calendar year. With this information, the first New Moon of the calendar year can be calculated and subsequent New Moons also.

Equator
A line that circles the earth at right angles to the Axis, and midway between the north and south poles – Declination is 0 degrees

Equinoxes
The intersections of the Ecliptic with the Celestial Equator

Great Year
This is the complete precession of the equinoxes that takes 25,920 years

Gregorian Calendar

This calendar is actually a revised version of the Julian calendar. It is closer to accuracy because of an improved method of determining Leap Years. It was introduced in 1582 by the Catholic Priesthood.

Halakim

This is a Hebrew division of time that amounts to 3 1/3 seconds. There are 18 to a minute and 1080 to an hour.

Heliacal

Refers to a star rising or setting with the sun. *Heliacal Rising* indicates that the star will appear on the eastern horizon minutes before the light of the sun blots it from visibility. *Heliacal Setting* indicates that the star appears briefly on the western horizon at sunset, then immediately follows the sun below the western horizon.

Horizon

The line where the sky and earth seem to meet, in all directions, from the perspective of an observer looking into the distance

Intercalation

To insert a day or month into a calendar
See Appendix for more information

Julian Calendar

This is a calendar introduced in 46 BC that counted the Tropical year as 365.25 days, which is an error of about 11 minutes, hence the calendar was generally replaced by the Gregorian calendar in 1582.

Julian Period

Consecutive numbering of the days with the starting date set as January 1, 4713 BC. Not related to the Julian calendar. This system was establish to help circumvent the problem of trying to determine true historical dates that are otherwise referenced by regional or cultural calendars that may be confusing.

Latitude

Coordinate Lines that run parallel to the equator

Leap year

A year in which an adjustment is made to the calendar, by adding an extra day

LUNAR LEAP YEAR

A year in which a month is added to the lunar calendar in order to keep it in sync with the tropical calendar (seasons). The lunar year is about 11 days short of the tropical (solar) year, so this adjustment is made about every 3rd year.

Light Year

Distance traveled by light in one year. Light travels at 186,282 miles per second.

Line Of Apsides

A line connecting the Apogee and Perigee of the moons orbit. Makes a complete revolution in about 8.85 years

Longitude

Geographical coordinate Lines that run parallel to the Prime Meridian, measured from a line the runs north to south through Greenwich, England (designated 0 degrees longitude)

Lunations

This is the time that elapses between two new moon 29.530589 days, 29 days 12 hours 44 minutes 3 1/3 seconds

Meridian

Celestial line running north to south through both celestial Poles and the Zenith of the observer

Metonic Cycle

This is a cycle of 6939.688 days that is used to reconcile the Synodic month with the Tropical year. It contains 19 Tropical years and 235 Lunations.

See Appendix for more information.

Molad

Hebrew term that indicates the astronomical point of the New Moon, that is the instant when the moon's angle to the sun has been reduced to zero degrees. Molad means rebirth.

Months (Lunar)

TROPICAL

Interval of time between transiting the same celestial longitude – 27.32156 days

SIDEREAL

Interval of time between transiting a Star – 27.32166 days

SYNODIC

Interval of time between alignment with the sun a zero degrees difference in angle – 29.530589 days

DRACONIAN

Interval of time between the transit of the nodes – 27.2122 days

Nadir

The point directly below the observer extended into Space

Nile River

The Lifeline of Egypt, for all practical purposes the only source of water for the land of Egypt. Savior. The Inundation occurs about the time of the Summer Solstice with flooding that lasts for about 4 months, the water level is moderate for about 4 months and low for about 4 months.

Nodes
Points of intersection of the apparent orbital paths of the sun and the moon

Nodical Cycle
This is a Cycle of 6793.5049 days, 18.61 solar years, 230 Lunations. The time it takes for the nodes to make a complete revolution. The position of the nodes shift about 19 1/3 degrees a year (18.6 days). The Eclipse year is 18.6 days shorter than the Tropical year.
See Appendix for more information

North Celestial Pole (NCP)
The Point of the geographical North Pole extended into the cosmos

North Pole
A point 90 degrees north of the equator – the northern end of the earth's axis of rotation

Orbit
The Path that a celestial body follows as it revolves around another celestial body. The orbit is maintained by the gravitational Pull of the Parent celestial body.

Parsec
206,265 astronomical units

Paschal Cycle

This is a cycle of 532 years. The cycle is a product of multiplying the Solar Cycle (28 years) time the Metonic Cycle (19 years). The Solar Cycle repeats the same correlation of *dates with days* after 28 years. The Metonic Cycle reconciles the lunar month with the tropical year after 19 years (6939.6017 days) verses 235 Lunations (6939.6884 days). The result is that after 532 years the phases of the moon will repeat on the same days/dates. In other words the Epact of the moon on January 1st will be the same as it was 532 years prior; that is, assuming the use of a calendar that approximates 365.25 days and 7-day weeks.

Perigee

Point in the moon's orbit that is closest to the earth

Perihelion

Point in the earth's orbit that is closest to the sun

Precession Of The Equinoxes

This is the gradual westward movement of the position of the equinoxes. The position of the equinox moves west by about 1/72 of a degree each year. For this reason, the Tropical year is shorter than the Sidereal year by about 20 minutes and 24 seconds.

The Following graphic illustrates the effect of the precession of the equinoxes. **The graphic is not drawn to scale**, in fact it is *Extremely exaggerated* so that we may clearly show how precession effects the length of the Tropical year. **VE** stands for the Vernal Equinox which marks the beginning of spring (the tropical year). The **star** represents any distant star that the astronomers may use to mark the alignment of the sun as it makes it's *apparent* crossing of the equinox. Assume that the earth's yearly revolution starts at point **A** and moves counterclockwise to point **A2** – that distance is a solar year of 365.242199 days. The distance counterclockwise from point **A** around to **A** again is a sidereal year of 365.2564 days. The span from point **A** to **A2** is the westward shifting of the point of equinox (precession) made in one year that is 1/72 degree of arc. It takes 25,920 years for the precession to complete 360 degrees.

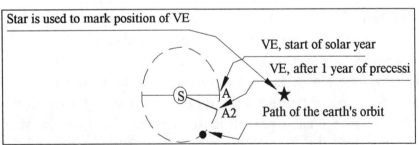

Star is used to mark position of VE

VE, start of solar year

VE, after 1 year of precessi

Path of the earth's orbit

Figure 10: Earth revolves counterclockwise. A to A2 is the Tropical yr - 365 days 5 hrs 48 min 45.51 sec. A to A again is the Sidereal yr - 365 days 6 hrs 9 min 9.54 sec. The span between A2 and A marks the precession of the equinoxes in 1 yr (1/72 deg)

Prime Meridian

Celestial line running north to south through both celestial Poles and directly above 0 degrees earth longitude

Revolve

The action of a celestial body orbiting another celestial body

Right Ascension

The angular measurement eastward from the vernal equinox. Lines of Right Ascension are at right angles to the celestial equator.

Rotation

The action of a celestial body turning about it's own Axis

Saros Cycle

A cycle of 6585.621124 days, 18.03 solar (365.242199 days) years, 19 eclipse (346.641124 days) years, 223 Lunations (29.530589 days), 242 Draconic (27.2122 days) months. It contains a series of 70 eclipses (41 solar and 29 lunar) Commences with a New Moon and continues until the New Moon returns to the same position. i.e. 18 years 11 1/3 days.

See Appendix for more information

Solar Cycle

This is a Calendar cycle of 28 years, whereas after a period of 28 years the days of the 7 day week return to the same dates. This assumes a calendar year of 365.25 days. If not for the Leap Year, the cycle would be completed in 7 years.

Solstices

The maximum and minimum Declinations of the sun –plus 23.5 degrees at the Summer Solstice and minus 23.5 degrees at the Winter Solstice

Sothic Cycle

An Egyptian cycle of 1460 years connected to the star Sirius as a marker. If the tropical year of approximately 365 ¼ days is counted as 365 days – the ¼ day discrepancy will grow to a complete year of 365 days in 1460 years, at which time the calendar could be reconciled by adding one full year to the date.

See appendix for more information

South Celestial Pole (SCP)

The Point of the geographical South Pole extended into the cosmos

South Pole

A point 90 degrees south of the equator – the southern end of the earth's axis of rotation

Tilt of the Earth's Axis to the Plane of it's orbit

The Earth Axis is tilted at an angle of 23.45 degrees, and this causes Altitude of the sun to oscillate between 23.45 degrees north Declination and 23.45 degrees south Declination during the course of one year. The Axis is tilted toward the sun at the summer solstice. The Axis is tilted away from the sun at the winter solstice. The sun is above the equator at the equinoxes.

Tropic Of Cancer
Region that extends to 23.45 degrees north of the equator, limit of the suns northerly declination

Tropic Of Capricorn
Region that extends to 23.45 degrees south of the equator, limit of the suns southerly declination

Years
TROPICAL

The time required for one complete revolution of the earth about the sun relative to the vernal equinox – 365 days 5 hours 48 minutes 45.51 seconds (365.2421 days)

SIDEREAL

The time required for one complete revolution of the earth about the sun, relative to a fixed star – 365 days 6 hours 9 minutes 9.54 seconds (365.2564 days)

ANOMALISTIC

The interval of time between the sun transiting the Perihelion – 365 days 6 hours 13 minutes 53.1 seconds (365.2596 days)

ECLIPSE

The interval of time between the sun transiting the nodes –
346.642199 days

SYNODIC

A year of 12 Lunations – 354.36708 days

Zenith

The point directly above the observer extended into Space

Index